1st Edition, July 2015
Copyright © 2015 Dimitris Michas
All Rights Reserved
ISBN: 978-960-93-7077-6

Contact:
e-mail: info@thegameofpersuasion.com
http://www.thegameofpersuasion.com

DIMITRIS MICHAS

The Game of Persuasion

36 ways to influence your audience

EXPERIENCES FROM SPEECHES OF THE MOST SUCCESSFUL CEOs

4

Table of Contents

Introduction

Over the centuries, people's ability to speak in a consistent, smooth and impressive manner provided them with opportunities to appear before an audience and wield their charm over the latter with their speech. These people were known as "orators", and their art became known as "rhetoric." Rhetoric or better rhetoric art is one of the arts of using language as a means to persuade. Rhetoric is a set of guidelines or rules that can be taught and if complied with, the likelihood of succeeding as an orator is greater. Along with grammar and logic (or dialectic), rhetoric is one of the three ancient arts of discourse. From ancient Greece to the late 19th century, it played an important role in Western education, while the art of defining a meaning was a central part of rhetoric, appearing in the "Themes" of Aristotle (Kennedy, 1991).

Rhetoric though has also another meaning; that is the acquired or innate human ability to perform spoken discourse in a pleasing and convincing manner. How a person can captivate their audience with their eloquence and ultimately to control it, has never failed to impress, from the first leaders of a tribe to the various kings and emperors, and from the first politicians, public speakers and thinkers to contemporary political talented writers with their staff and the CEOs of major companies, such as those discussed below. This book examines extensively the art of rhetoric as taught and learned, but also rhetoric as a speaker's skill.

The book focuses on creating a theoretical framework of 36 point-criteria for assessing the influence of the speakers and their speech on an audience. What makes thus a speech good or bad and a speaker effective or not? The book attempts to analyze what a speech usually focuses on, depending on the subject and objectives of the speech and more specifically, those elements of the speech directly related to the management of human resources. Subsequently, after the creation of this theoretical framework, the book will analyze speeches given by prominent executives of large corporations in order to apply the theoretical framework to the analysis of selected speeches, by identifying and comparing the data provided. Finally, this book focuses on those elements of a business speech given by senior managers that are used to influencing managerial staff and other employees to whom the speech is addressed.

The methodology followed in the first stage concerns the analysis of the broad literature on rhetoric, the power and influence of rhetorical persuasion, the power and importance of rhetoric in corporate human resource management and it relates to the theoretical framework which the proposed material will later be compared to.

The techniques used for the analysis of the speeches are Content Analysis and Discourse Analysis. By analyzing the content, I was able to measure quantitatively how many times some keywords appeared and with discourse analysis I qualitatively analyzed the speeches themselves, trying to draw conclusions from the speech as a whole and not just from certain keywords. Content analysis is a quantitative technique, which probably cannot fully grasp the meaning of the language that is developing through the speech. It is rather an additional tool for my analysis, which helps to prove some important points and arguments made in the book. It cannot be used as the sole or primary means of analysis nor the only technique for the analytical purposes of this book, due to the false conclusions that the mere presentation of quantitative findings may produce. Therefore, it is necessarily accompanied by an essential qualitative technique, discourse analysis, in order to present accurately the correctly targeted research findings (Bryman, 2004).

In both cases, the words and meanings chosen for the quantitative analysis of the content and the qualitative analysis of discourse are based on the following theoretical framework and have been chosen in order to pinpoint interesting and targeted information for the best possible and comprehensive analysis of the above problem; the impact and influence of corporate rhetoric on the management of human resources.

The criteria used for selecting the speeches were the position of the speaker and of the company, as only CEOs of major companies were chosen. I have therefore received a satisfactory sample of ten (10) total different speeches of CEOs in order to attain a numerically adequate sample of analysis without it becoming too large and cumbersome. Additionally, the speeches are addressed to company executives and future executives (university graduates) in order to highlight the relationship between corporate rhetoric and the management of human resources.

For the selection of companies and their CEOs, I consulted the reliable and distinguished list in Forbes magazine which features the 10 largest companies in the world based on their market value. The ten largest companies in 2014 based on their market value were: 1) Apple, 2) Exxon Mobil, 3) Google, 4) Microsoft, 5) Berkshire Hathaway, 6) Johnson & Johnson, 7) Wells Fargo, 8) General Electric, 9) Roche Holding and 10) Wal-Mart Stores.

Thus, from this list I chose the following active CEOs of these companies, whose speeches I have analyzed below (except for Apple's Steve Jobs and Microsoft's Bill Gates that were selected over the current (2014) CEOs Tim Cook and Satya Nadella, respectively, due to the extent and global influence of their personalities): 1) **Steve Jobs**, Stanford University Commencement Address, 2005 (Apple), 2) **Rex Tillerson**, Meeting the Energy Challenges of the Future: The Role of Industry and Government, 2014 (Exxon Mobil), 3) **Larry Page**, University of Michigan Commencement Address, 2009 (Google), 4) **Bill Gates**, Microsoft Research Faculty Summit, 2013 (Microsoft), 5) **Warren Buffett**, SALOMON INC – A report by the Chairman on the Company's Position and Outlook, 1991 (Berkshire Hathaway), 6) **Alex Gorsky**, National Academy Foundation, 2014 (Johnson & Johnson), 7) **John Stumpf**, Q2 2014 Results, 2014 (Wells Fargo), 8) **Jeff Immelt**, General Electric's new center will create 1,100 jobs in Detroit, 2009 (General Electric), 9) **Severin Schwan**,

Annual General Meeting Roche Holding Ltd, 2011 (Roche Holding) and 10) **Doug Mcmillon**, Picking up the Pace of Change for the Customer, 2014 (Wal-Mart).

I. Corporate Rhetoric and its Influence

A. Means and Tools of Persuasion

1. Morality, Passion and Reason

Aristotle talked about three different types of mental evidence used by persuasive speakers: 1) Morality - Ethos (moral-character and reputation), 2) Passion (reliance on emotion) and 3) Reason (reliance on logic).

Morality or **Ethos** concerns the speaker's character, as revealed through communication. It is mostly built over a long period of time and not only during a single speech, without this entailing that it cannot be supported by that speech.

So, in order to create credibility the speaker should initially be consistent in his speech with the words and deeds before the speech, and thus unnatural and excessive courtesy to the public (in order to create sympathy, as discussed below) in combination with authoritarianism with the same audience (as employees) at other times, may be crucially damaging as regards credibility. Subsequently, during the speech the truth should not be concealed from the audience without either withholding bad news (but rather to conceal them with the "art of comparison" as discussed below), excessive promises should not be made that will later affect the speaker's reliability if later not kept,. Finally, a speaker can retrieve lost credibility, by acknowledging mistakes and by correcting them later (Baldoni, 2003).

Hyland (1998) states that CEOs generally try to project a positive image of themselves and of the company using phrases that guide the audience towards understanding the way they want the alleged subject to be put across, generating feelings of confidence and trust in their employees, shareholders, regulatory agencies, financial media and the public in general (Aristotle's ethos). Thus, we have a rhetorical product that can have a significant impact on the competitive position of the company (Kohut & Segars, 1992). Very often the projections of a successful image may be even more important than the needs of the audience for accurate and useful information (Cross, 1990).

Passion has to do with the feelings of the audience and how a speech can create an emotional connection [1]. It therefore concerns appealing to the listeners' senses (with techniques such as including personal experiences) generating appropriate feelings of sadness, surprise, disgust, anger, happiness or fear.

Finally, **Reason** refers to logic, i.e. the words used by the speaker. The choice of words and the use of narratives, sayings or references to events all play an important role in shifting the audience towards the desired direction. For Aristotle, the primary element of the three is reason followed by ethos and passion, but nowadays ethos is perhaps the most important of the three, because of the need people have to ensure the validity and ethics of the individual speaker before they identify and connect with their logical and sentimental arguments (Borg, 2007).

2. Visual, Auditory and Verbal Rhetoric

The art of persuasion according to Borg (2007, p.23) refers to any message that focuses and aims to influence the opinion, attitude or actions of people, and in particular the sincerity of the speakers and the connection they have with the public.

According to Borg (2007, pp 26-27), for a speaker to be able to appeal to the public, he should possess two kinds of intelligence: interpersonal intelligence, i.e. the ability to understand the feelings and anticipate the reactions of the public and intrapersonal intelligence, i.e. the ability to fully understand their own mental processes, and the reasons why they occur.

In the `60s, Los Angeles University professor, Albert Mehrabian, after a considerable research and a series of experiments concluded that 55% of the impact of the message of a speaker is visual (i.e. the image of the speaker), 38% is auditory (the volume of the voice (i.e. the intensity of certain words used), the pace of the speech (very fast pace can be incomprehensible and very slow pace can be tiring), the intonation of the voice (low or high, such as when there is a question), the hue and the variation of the voice (i.e. the skillful use of the change of the tone of the voice to suit the occasion and the message the speaker wants) and only 7% is verbal (words themselves, what he says and how he says it).

As far as **visual persuasion is concerned**, apart from the overall appearance of the speaker (dress, how good looking they are etc.), equally important is the posture of the speaker at the time of the speech (without excessive body movements that might give the impression of anxiety (which is transmitted to the public)), while it is much easier to hook the public's attention if the speaker knows his speech by heart and does not read it (and therefore has a constant visual contact with his audience), provided that this can be done smoothly and without efforts to remember what they want to say. Therefore, speakers should show confidence, as if they "owned the hall," to be upright and not to take a defensive position with their body (crossed hands and feet) and to use their hands only when needed (excessive use may be considered negative) (Pease, 2004).

As far as **auditory persuasion is concerned**, it is important that the speaker does not speak neither too fast nor too slowly and to exploit pauses during the speech (e.g. in the beginning to hook the attention of the audience), and use natural articulation, emphasizing the point intended to gain the public's attention, while retaining authenticity (Smith, 2013).

As far as **verbal persuasion is concerned**, Baldoni (2003) states that there are three stages. The first stage is the development and structure of the message, the second is the transmission of the message to the audience and the third is maintaining the message.

As regards the **development and structure of the message**, it should first confirm the objectives, vision and mission of the organization that the speaker represents, giving a sense of security in the audience, while the content should be related to the cause for which the speech was made. It should also take an initiative for change, calling the audience for action, while also giving the impression that it is has been made exclusively for them (in order to answer the question "What do I win?" from every individual in the audience). It should also be different, simple but not too simplistic, containing original and memorable short words and phrases that can gain public attention for their originality (particularly if these words or phrases close the speech) and, finally, it should be repeated several times in order to be remembered by the public. The speaker should also inform the audience about the basic argument, remaining open to suggestions from the audience, giving them a sense of openness to the purpose and vision of himself/herself and of the organization s/he represents in order to make them think about their position and the future of the organization (Baldoni, 2003).

Regarding the **transmission of the message to the audience**, speakers should avoid unnecessary babble and large thanking openings, keep their speech short (under 20 minutes), remind the audience of shared experiences (if any), use their own authentic style, and deliver a "live" performance, but without copying other speakers. In addition, the use of sarcasm (especially self-sarcasm), though sometimes dangerous (since the sense of humor may differ), if indicated by the nature of the public and of the speech and if there is a possibility they might be successful, could prove to be very important in catching the public's attention as a part of the art of liking that I will analyze below. All these contribute to the authenticity and sincerity of the intentions of the speaker, building a closer relationship with the audience (Smith, Darlington, 2013, Baldoni, 2003).

Finally, as regards the **preservation of the message**, this part primarily entails keeping the public interested, which is achieved, as mentioned above, with the brevity of speech and the constant repetition of the main idea-message of the speaker. Similarly, the use of stories (mostly personal) contribute largely in keeping the public interested and in the ultimate success of the speech, as it is much easier to understand and later on remember a story. The stories make the audience think what they can achieve in the future, as stories are inherently focused on human capacity and condition (Baldoni, 2003).

Furthermore, in terms of speech content, the moderate use of statistics is useful, as they may not be retained by the audience, but they provide authority to the speaker, the art of which I will analyze below (Smith, 2013).

Using certain connective key phrases in a sentence can shift the interest of the audience where the speaker wants, as a form of hypnotic guidance. Examples of connecting phrases are mostly illustrated by connecting links such as 'because', 'and', and 'but' in order to shift the interest in the second sentence, particularly if the first sentence is preceded by the verb 'agree' so that there is the idea of condescension, whether this relates directly to the public or not (Basu, 2009).

Hyland (1998) refers to even more categories of connective links of verbal persuasion, indicating that such verbal connections can actually create preferred explanations of concepts proposed by the speakers. Therefore, such verbal connections help in forming a convincing and coherent text associating individual proposals together with the concept of the public. The various categories of verbal connections are: 1) logical verbal connections that lead to a realistic connection of concepts such as the aforementioned 'but', 'because', 'and', 'also' and 'so-therefore', 2) verbal connections of continuity such as 'first', 'second', 'after', 'finally' to help organize the processing by the audience and create a logical follow-up, 3) verbal connections of probability such as 'maybe', 'may', 'probably' that keep the speaker at a distance from an event or a proposal, 4) emphatic verbal connections such as 'in reality', 'definitely', 'certainly' that indicate the certainty of the speaker, 5) citing verbal connections 'according to', 'X said' usually referred to distinguished persons or sources and are used to give so-called 'objectivity' to the speaker and finally 6) emotional verbal links such as 'I', 'we', 'between us' that are used to create emotional connection with the audience (invoked Passion) (Hyland, 1998, pp 6-7).

In the research he conducted in 137 CEOs' speeches, he found that the verbal connections that were most often used were "and", "as well" and "but" with 13.3%, 9.4% and 4.6% respectively of the total verbal connections used (Hyland, 1998, p.12).

3. Techniques of Persuasion

As regards the various techniques used by speakers to convince the audience that focus on morality, passion and reason, Arizona University psychology professor, Robert Cialdini, addressing the then unfamiliar marketeers' audience of the 1980s, states in his classic book "Influence: the Psychology of Persuasion" that there are 7 basic tools of human influence. 1) The art of comparison, 2) The art of reciprocation, 3) The art of commitment and consistency, 4) The art of mimicry (social proof), 5) The art of liking, 6) The art of power and authority, and 7) the art of exclusivity (Cialdini, 1984).

The **art of comparison** refers to the creation of comparative examples, a process through which emerges the object under examination. The perspective from which the listener-viewer perceives various situations can change dramatically in terms of a specific topic [2] (Cialdini, 1984).

Thus, when many expensive identical objects are presented to a buyer and later on a cheaper one is presented, s/he will be tempted to buy it, while at the same time if they first present ugly objects and then a beautiful one, s/he will again be tempted to buy it (Cialdini, 1984).

Therefore, in this respect, a CEO presenting the profits or losses of a company or a new product, will strive to create comparative situations so that the audience will be affected to such an extent that losses will seem less important, profits will seem even more important, and products will look even better.

The **art of reciprocation** refers to the psychological condition created in a person to reciprocate a gift or a favor. If someone receives a birthday gift s/he will be forced to reciprocate on the birthday of the person who brought the gift. It is also an old trick used by Gypsies and other organizations to raise money by offering a flower or another 'gift' to a stranger walking in the street in order to force him/her to reciprocate by giving financial assistance to the 'donor'. The stranger will be faced with the following dilemma: either to reject the 'gift', something that is considered socially rude and many times difficult as the physical reaction to the sudden offer of an object demands to receive what was offered. Or to accept it and then reciprocate. There are a few cases where the stranger will receive it without reciprocating, but s/he is more likely to dump it in the next dustbin, from which it will be collected later by the same people to offer it to another stranger. A similar example is the testing of products in various shops and supermarkets by overly smiley staff, who apart from creating familiarity with the product, are targeting feelings of reciprocation in their customers who will be 'forced' to buy the product they tested, even though they did not particularly like it [3] (Cialdini, 1984).

Many times, the art of reciprocation leads to multiple benefits, as frequently the subject of the gift wants to offer more in return, and may well be combined with the art of comparison when subject A asks for something much larger than what subject B wants to give and will be forced to refuse, but when later on subject A asks for something comparatively smaller, subject B will be forced to give in to the request of subject A because 1) the second request seems comparatively smaller and 2) s/he will be forced to reciprocate for his/her rejection of the first request. Thus it can be said that the blending of the arts of comparison and reciprocation is the cornerstone of any negotiation (Cialdini, 1984).

Thus, with respect to our topic, a CEO is likely to use the art of reciprocation (such as promises for better working conditions) to create psychological conditions of reciprocation in his audience.

The **art of commitment and consistency** refers broadly to the need to be consistent. Thus, the player who bets on a horse in a race may be uncertain until the time s/he places the bet. From that moment on, he will support his choice and believe firmly that this was the right choice to make (or winning in this case) [4] (Cialdini, 1984).

Another example of the power of the art of commitment and consistency is research conducted for the American Association Against Cancer. Thus when a telephone survey conducted on households on whether they would supposedly volunteer to fundraising for fighting against cancer (creating without them knowing a commitment), preceded an actual visit from the Association to these households, the percentage of volunteers increased by 700% compared to the previous visit, prior to which there had been no telephone survey (Cialdini, 1984, p.68).

The art of commitment and consistency was widely used in Chinese concentration camps, where they captured Americans during the Korean War in the early 1950s. In exchange for food or cigarettes, the Chinese guards would ask their American captives to make some small –with their signature though- anti-American claims, such as: "America is not perfect," "In a communist regime there are no problems of unemployment" "America has problems like ... (and they would write what they thought)." These confessions signed by US soldiers were later used for propaganda purposes on the other prisoners and American soldiers at war. What may seem as a surprise, however, is the fact that since they signed the propaganda and were considered collaborators of the communist regime, and since they had not been tortured to write those statements, they argued passionately about them, trapped by the art of commitment and consistency (Cialdini, 1984, p. 71).

A CEO is likely to use the art of commitment and consistency to create conditions of psychological bonding with the audience, or in order to prove his

Aristotelian ethos indicating his consistency to previous commitments.

The **art of mimicry or social proof** refers to the human need to look to other people and try to find examples of how to behave [5] (Cialdini, 1984).

The art of social proof arises from the principle that 95% of people imitate other people and only 5% are real pioneers and thus finds fertile ground mainly in the uncertainty that people feel in their lives, seeking impatiently the 'right' move in other people's actions (Cialdini, 1984, p.118).

When it became known in the news that a woman was murdered by a man while hunting her for half an hour, the audience was particularly struck only when informed that during this half an hour there were 38 witnesses, none of whom took action and did not call the police. With everyone believing that someone else would help and call the police and at the same time watching each other doing nothing, the principle of social proof dictated that no one should take action [6] (Cialdini, 1984, p.129).

It has also been proven that after a suicide made headlines, the number of suicides and accident in general increased by 1000% in the next few days, suggesting that people who had problems and had contemplated suicide, found a pattern to imitate directly, or indirectly to drive their vehicle into a fatal accident (Cialdini, 1984, p.144).

A CEO is likely to use the art of mimicry or social proof to acquire (or in most cases by having already placed in the audience) supporters, with these supporters causing others to imitate them in order to embrace the views and words of the speaker. In addition, s/he can give successful examples of himself, 'pointing' to an example worthy of copying.

The **art of liking** refers to the increased ability of persuasion that is shown by someone who is likeable to the audience [7] (Cialdini, 1984).

A key physical feature that makes someone 'likable' are external features, i.e. how attractive the speaker is. Several studies have shown that when someone is handsome automatically they are also characterized as 'gifted', 'kind', 'honest' and 'smart' (Cialdini, 1984, p.171).

Another feature that makes a speaker likeable to the audience is how 'similar' he appears to be to his audience. This similarity does not only refer to physical characteristics, but also as regards aspects of character and behavior and, finally, a speaker is likeable, when s/he makes compliments to his/her audience (Cialdini, 1984).

Thus, with respect to our topic, a CEO is likely to use the art of liking to become likeable to the public, often by adopting a similar dress code (only where this similar dress code does not conflict with the art of authority, as discussed below (business environment) or when the speaker is a well-known figure (Steve Jobs)), or by making compliments to the public (e.g. you are the best in...) and adopting a manner of speech and a vocabulary close to the audience, and in most cases being rather attractive.

The **art of power and authority** is perhaps the most important art that a speaker can adopt. It derives from the idea that someone who has influence and power over others (captain of his soldiers, manager to his subordinates, etc.) or has an intellectual authority (a teacher over their students, a doctor to their patients, etc.), has a great influence over their audience, to the extent that they may not only respect and obey their words, but could even kill in order to obey their orders, and many times that obedience reaches the limits of annihilation of personal judgment, as shown by the famous experiment of psychology professor Stanley Milgram [8], while people also think that the person-authority is 2.5 to 7 cm taller than they actually are. Milgram summed up the experiment of 1974 in his article, "The Dangers of Obedience", writing that: "The legal and philosophic aspects of obedience are of enormous importance, but they say very little about how most people behave in concrete situations. I set up a simple experiment at Yale University to check how much pain an ordinary citizen may cause to another person simply because he was ordered to by an experimental scientist. The principle of power-authority was faced with the powerful moral barriers of participants who had their ears filled with the screams of the victims, with the principle of power-authority to win more often than not. The extreme willingness of adults to follow almost every command of an authority constitutes the main finding of the study and the fact that calls urgently for an explanation. Ordinary people, simply doing their jobs and without any particular hostility on their part can become agents in a terrible and destructive process. Moreover, even when the destructive effects of their actions are quite clear to them, and they are invited to perform actions incompatible with their fundamental standards of morality, relatively few people have the moral courage required to resist this power" (Milgram, 1974).

Milgram later created two theories about the causes of obedience to authority. One is the theory of conformism, in which a person, who has neither the ability nor the experience to make decisions, especially in a crisis, will leave the decision making process to the group and its hierarchy. The group is thus the behavioral model of the individual. The second focuses on the theory of relieving the responsibility of the subject and says that the essence of obedience consists in the fact that the subject sees himself as the instrument for carrying out the wishes of another person and, therefore, is no longer completely responsible for his actions. So once this critical shift of renunciation of responsibility in the subject is completed, obedience occurs (Milgram, 1974).

Even religion can play a role in this exaggeration of the principle of power-authority, with the Bible, for example, to indicate how the failure of obedience to authority resulted in the loss of Paradise for Adam and Eve (Cialdini, 1984, p.217).

Thus, a CEO is likely to use the art of power and authority to influence their audience, wearing business suits (social and professional superiority) and overall trying to give the impression that they know several topics in depth (e.g. using statistics).

Finally, the **art of scarcity** refers to the ability of the speaker to artificially create the impression of exclusivity, either in terms of his/her presence or his/her words, with the aim of creating the image that only a selected few have the privilege to hear him/her [9].

Therefore a CEO is likely to use the art of scarcity to influence the public, giving the impression of exclusivity as regards his/her appearance or of sayings uttered to create and combine this exclusivity with the charm of a forbidden fruit.

Notes

[1] The ability to decipher and understand the feelings, ideas and positions of others.

[2] In an experiment, the volunteer put one hand in a bucket of hot water and the other in a bucket of iced water. When he placed them at the same time in a bucket of lukewarm water, he observed the following phenomenon: The hand that was in the bucket with hot water suddenly felt that the water was icy cold and the hand that was in the bucket with ice water felt that the water in the bucket was hot, when in both cases it was water of the same temperature (Cialdini, 1984).

[3] An example of the art of reciprocation is a German soldier of the First World War, who captured an enemy soldier while eating, and while he was about to execute him, the prisoner made a move that would save his life: he offered some of his food to the German soldier. Driven by feelings of reciprocation, he did not kill him, but instead left (Cialdini, 1984).

[4] In an experiment that carried out by the psychologist Thomas Moriarty, the researcher studied 20 people who witnessed the following

incident: a swimmer left his bag before he went bathing and it was later on stolen by a passerby. Out of 20 people, only 4 chased the thief. In a second experiment with exactly the same conditions, he asked each person (the research subject) to watch over his things before entering the sea. Driven by a sense of consistency (in this case, their word that they will pay attention to the things of the unknown swimmer) and the fact that inconsistency is not socially acceptable, this time 19 out of 20 people chased the thief, revealing the power of the art of commitment and consistency (Cialdini, 1984).

[5] A classic example of the art of social proof, and its need is (usually in American comedies and shows) canned laughter. Despite the fact that it is easily recognizable by the vast majority as artificial laughter, the audience find shows containing it funnier. A similar example is - common in traditional theaters and opera houses over the centuries - the use of paid people (claquers and their coordinators, chef de claque) to be among spectators in order to clap and cheer during the performances, so that the other spectators would consider that the show was actually very good. Another example of the art of social proof are the half-full fundraising boxes, which may have just been installed, but in order to make other people deposit money, often the same people who collect the money would place some of their own money in order to invest in the art of social proof that would "oblige" people to act as 'others' (but who often simply do not exist) (Cialdini, 1984).

[6] In an experiment conducted in a psychiatric clinic for young children who feared dogs, it was proven that only the projection of a 20 minute video every day with children playing with dogs was enough to change their perspective and 67% of children would say after a few days that they would like to play with dogs. Also, in another experiment, a wallet with money and cards lying abandoned on a street in New York in a folder, contained a note which was written in such a way so as to imply that someone had found the wallet and was about to post it to the owner, but had also lost it. The experiment took place with two variations. In the first case the note was written in English with grammatical errors, suggesting that it was written by a foreigner, while in the second case in

fluent English, suggesting an American. In the first case, only 33% of wallets were returned, while in the second case 70%, suggesting that the principle of social proof has more weight when people think they are copying someone more alike to them (Cialdini, 1984).

[7] A classic example of the use of the art of liking occurs during the interrogation of detainees in police stations, with police officers attempting to gain a confession, the famous art of a bad and good cop. One suspect is interrogated by two police officers (either simultaneously or alternately), with the one being rude and verbally and physically violent towards the suspect. He is swearing, kicking everything he finds in his way, threatening to send him to prison for many years. The other allegedly tries to calm him down, finding excuses for the act for which the person is charged (for example, if it is a simple robbery, the fact that there were no casualties or if the robber had no gun, or whether he is young), while asking from the 'bad' cop, with some kind of excuse, to leave the interrogation room and leave him alone with the suspect. He will then try to show some kind of understanding for his actions and will offer some kind of reduced sentence as a 'good' cop and a 'friend'. The whole process is repeated with the two police officers with greater intensity, until the 'good' cop gains a confession, having used the art of liking (Cialdini, 1984).

[8] The Professor of Psychology at Yale, Stanley Milgram in 1961 created a psychological experiment in order to discover to what extent the average person (generally selected individuals with different social, academic and economic characteristics, in order for a society average to somehow appear), would obey orders coming from some kind of authority. Thus he searched for volunteers for a learning experiment, to be paid $4 for an hour of their time (good amount of money at the time). He involved three people: one who ran the experiment, one who was the subject of the experiment (volunteer), and an actor pretending to be a volunteer. These three people had three distinct roles: the Experimenter (the power-authority), the Teacher (volunteer intended to obey the orders of experimenter), and the Learner (the actor-recipient of stimulus from the Teacher). The roles of the Teacher and the Learner

were supposedly distributed by lots, but both lots wrote 'Teacher' and the actor would say every time that he had the role of the Learner. At this point, 'Teacher' and 'Learner' were put into different rooms where they could communicate but not see each other. In one version of the experiment, the actor-learner would report to the participant that he had a problem with his heart and started complaining after a while that he was exhausted and that he was not feeling well (so that the teacher-volunteer knew that the procedure could kill the Learner). The teacher received an electric shock from the shock generator as a sample of the shock that the learner was supposed to receive during the experiment. The teacher was then given a list of word-pairs to 'teach' the student to memorize. The teacher began by reading the list of words to the learner. He read the first word of each pair and the four possible answers. The learner would have to press a button to indicate his response. If the answer was incorrect, the teacher turned a switch transmitting an electric shock to the learner, with the voltage increasing 15-volt for each wrong answer. If the answer was correct, the teacher would read the next word pair. The teacher therefore believed that for each wrong answer, the learner was receiving a real electric shock. In reality, however, there were no shocks. On a tape they played recorded sounds for each shock level. After a series of wrong answers and corresponding increases in voltage, the learner-actor began striking the wall that separated him from the teacher. After several times hitting the wall and complaining about the state of his heart, he stopped giving answers to the questions of teacher (supposedly trying to show that he was unable to answer). At this point, many volunteers expressed their desire to stop the experiment and check the student. After 135 volts many began to question the purpose of the experiment. Most of them continued after being reassured that they will not be held responsible for whatever happened. Some people began to laugh nervously or exhibit other signs of extreme stress once they heard the screams of pain coming from the learner. If at any time the volunteer expressed his desire to stop the experiment, he was given a series of verbal orders from the experimenter, in this order: 1) Please continue. 2) The experiment requires that you continue. 3) It is absolutely essential that you continue. 4) You have no choice, you must continue. If the volunteer still wanted to stop after all four successive verbal commands, the experiment was stopped. Otherwise, it stopped when the teacher had channeled the maximum shock of 450-volt three times consecutively to the learner. The experimenters also gave concrete answers if the teacher made specific comments. If the teacher asked whether the student may suffer permanent physical damage, the experimenter replied, "Although the shocks may be painful, there is no permanent tissue damage, please continue." If the teacher said that the learner clearly wants to stop, the experimenter replied, "whether the learner likes it or not, you should continue until he has learned all the word pairs correctly, so please continue." Prior to conducting the experiment, Milgram asked fourteen senior psychology students at Yale University to estimate the behavior of 100 volunteers with the role of the 'Teacher'. The respondents believed that only a very small percentage of 'teachers' (the range was from 0-3 to 100, with an average 1.2) could cause the maximum shock. Milgram also did an informal survey on his colleagues and found that they believed that very few would go beyond a very strong shock. Milgram also asked 40 psychiatrists from a medical school, who believed that after the tenth electric shock when the victim would require to be set free, most volunteers would stop the experiment. They predicted that after the shock of 300V, when the victim refused to respond, only 3.73 percent of the volunteers would continue, and believed that "only a little more than one tenth of one percent of the volunteers would proceed to the maximum electric shock of 450V". In the first series of experiments of Milgram, 65 percent (26 of 40) of participants in the experiment proceeded to the 450V shock of the experiment, although many felt very uncomfortable doing it so. At some point, all the participants did pause and question the experiment. Some said they would return the money they were paid for their participation in the experiment. Throughout the experiment, the volunteers exhibited varying degrees of tension and stress. They exhibited sweating, trembling, stuttering, they bit their lips, hurt their skin with their fingernails and some of them had nervous laughter, convulsions or seizures. None, however, from the participants who did not proceed to the last electric shocks insisted that the experiment itself had to be terminated, nor left the room to check the health of the victim without

31

first asking for permission to leave. Thomas Blass from the University of Maryland, conducting a meta-analysis of the results from repeated experiments and found that the proportion of participants who are ready to cause lethal voltages remains remarkably stable, 61-66 percent, regardless of time or place. Also, in other experiments conducted by Milgram later, he connected and isolated even more the power of authority as the main cause of obedience. In one experiment, the students were supposedly brave enough that despite the pain, asked from the teacher to continue. As a result 100% refused to continue and proceeded to the request of the student when there was no command from the experimenter, and later, after changing roles, with the experimenter being the learner and the learner giving orders, nobody pulled the lever. In another experiment there were two experimenters who were present, but disagreed on one aspect of the experiment as to whether the teacher-volunteer should continue delivering further shocks, with each one giving different orders whether to proceed or not. As a result, all volunteers followed their instincts and did not pull the lever (Milgram, 1974).

[9]A relevant example is the Shakespearian love between Romeo and Juliet whose love would have probably never reached high levels (let alone reach the point of suicide in the very idea of losing one another), if it was not for the family and social barriers that kept them apart and forbade them to be together, the forbidden fruit in the biblical narrative (Cialdini, 1984).

B. Corporate Rhetoric and HRM

A very important part of the HRM planning in any organization is rewarding human resources. Thus, one of the goals of corporate rhetoric is the indirect reward of the workforce. The reward is essentially a form of compensation for the worker's participation in the effort to fulfill the objectives of the organization (Papalexandri-Bourantas, 2013, p.377).

On the whole remuneration policies are used to engender a sense of motivation, responsibility and commitment in workers, they are the key driver in attracting and retaining employees, and in many cases they are the main reason for the increase in productivity (Papalexandri-Bourantas, 2013, pp 377-382).

Thus, rewards policies can take the classic form of a money-based incentive, but motivation may also take the form of interesting work, good working conditions and promotion opportunities. Other types of incentives can take the form of professional development provision and improving performance or skills. These incentives may be granted to the group or individual. Another category of incentives focuses on a worker's emotional state, such as acknowledging the employee's performance, creativity in the work field, confidence expressed towards subordinates by those at the top, and the prospects for personal development and advancement (Kartakoullis, 2013).

It is therefore easy to understand that mental rewards that can be given through corporate rhetoric can lead to better results for the company, by using psychological stimulation and motivation of employees. Thus, with respect to the remuneration of the company's human resources, corporate rhetoric plays a double role: it psychologically rewards employees by motivating them to work even harder and effectively, creates the best possible image of leadership, working conditions and the company's objectives, while also motivating those who do not work for the company by improving the company's image.

On numerous occasions corporate rhetoric can 'soften' the harsh and impersonal treatment of the superiors towards the employees, which constitutes the overall strategic plan of each company, treating their staff as units and components of a large mechanism (hard model), with the managing director-speaker trying to make them feel as essential partners in the company's vision, a 'conditio sine qua non' for the company's future (soft model), without giving a contradictory picture of himself (hard in work, pleasant in speech), which could undermine his credibility (morality) (Gill, 1999).

Therefore, the vocabulary regarding HRM may be regarded as an attempt to 'legitimize' managerial power, to redefine the rights of workers and to redraw the borders of control through a language that promotes reciprocity and shared commitment (Blyton & Turnbull, 1994).

Finally, corporate rhetoric in relation to HRM has to do with the emphasis on treating employees as assets and as a source of competitive advantage through their commitment, adaptability, high quality skills and performance. Employees are therefore dynamic rather than passive inputs in production processes and can be developed, are worthy of trust and cooperation. All of this can be achieved through their participation in the strategic plan of the corporate mechanism, thus enabling them to improve their position and the future of the organization. The objective of corporate rhetoric is therefore to create a kind of engagement through communication, motivation and leadership. The focus thus becomes the 'individual' (Legge, 1995).

C. The 36 Point-Criteria Theoretical Framework of Analysis

For the analysis of the following speeches I observed and assessed, in the light of the above, specific rhetorical tools that are widely used in speeches, in order to judge their effectiveness in connecting with HRM and more specifically whether the psychological reward and psychological encouragement of the workers occurs.

Thus, by analyzing each speech separately and in combination at the end, I evaluated the visual, auditory and verbal techniques of the speaker, whether the above techniques are used in speech, to what extent and how successfully.

By completing the analysis of visual, auditory and verbal techniques, but also of the whole content of the speech, I have drawn conclusions as to how effective the speech was, whether the speaker was convincing and to what extent he used the above research points, providing statistics and qualitative and quantitative examples and an overall assessment of the speech, with an explanation of the **36-point Influence Indicator of a Speaker** and how it is connected to HRM.

My analysis is therefore based both on the overall estimation of the speeches and their relationship with HRM and Verbal, Auditory and Verbal Persuasion (which contain all the theoretical points discussed above) for which each speaker was assessed and rated, adding a maximum of 10 points for every positive point and subtracting by a maximum of 10 points for every negative aspect, giving a total of 340 points in order to have a comparative measure of influence of the speeches on the audience and their employees and hence, mutatis mutandis, of the importance and success of any speech in attaining the aforementioned objectives of HRM.

The 36-point Influence Indicator of a Speaker

Visual Persuasion

Appearance (+10)
Dress (Close to the audience's [Art of Liking], Professional [Art of Authority]) (+10)
Body Position and Gestures (+10)
Arms and Legs Position and Moves (+10)

Continuous Contact with the audience (Does not read the speech) (+10)

Auditory Persuasion

Speed and Pace of Talking (+10)
Volume (+10)
Exploitation of Pauses (+10)
Articulation (+10)
Intonation (+10)

Verbal Persuasion

Morality:

Consistency with what he said in the Past (Art of Consistency) (+10)
Recognition of errors and correction (+10)

Speech Content and Main Message:

Confirm Goals, Vision and Mission of the Organization (+10)
Comparison of successes and failures for the benefit of the speaker and the company (Art of Comparison) (+10)
Relevance of Speech to its Topics and Goals (+10)
The Audience is at the center of the Speech ("What could I earn?" Promises for better working conditions, future-

benefits for the company, references to the, 'employees', 'partners' and 'stakeholders' [Art of Reciprocation]) (+10)
Initiative for change (+10)
Call for Action (+10)
Simplicity of speech (+10)
Originality of phrases and words used (Art of Scarcity) (+10)
Repetition of the main message (+10)

Transmission and Retention of the Message:

Babbling (thanking too much etc.) (-10)
Shortness of speech (+10)
Theatricality (Too much, reasonable) (-10, +10)
Compliments to the Audience (Art of Liking, Art of Reciprocation) (+10)
Failed Jokes (-10)
Successful Jokes (Art of Scarcity) (+10)
Self-sarcasm (+10)
Use of Stories and Examples (Social Proof, Art of Scarcity) (+10)

Verbal Content and Linking Phrases:

Statistics (too many, reasonable [Art of Authority]) (-10, +10)

Logical Verbal Links ('but', 'because', 'also', 'and', 'so') (+10)

Verbal Sequencing Links ('firstly', 'secondly', 'in addition', 'finally') (+10)

Verbal Links of Probability ('maybe', 'possibly', 'probably') (+10)

Emphatic Verbal Links ('in reality', 'certainly', 'definitely') (+10)

Citing Verbal Links ('according to', 'X said') (+10)

Emotional Verbal Links ('I', 'we', 'between us') (+10)

Overall Degree of Speaker's Influence: = [- 40 (min.), 340 (max.)]

II. CEOs' Speeches and their Influence in HRM

Steve Jobs (Apple)

The speech given by Steve Jobs at Stanford in 2005 has been described as one of the most influential speeches of all time and perhaps the most successful from a CEO.

It was addressed to graduate students in their graduation ceremony (prospective or existing employees), it succeeds in conveying three simple, clear and consistent messages to the public that focus (regarding HRM) mainly on encouraging the public and less on rewarding it (something which is reasonable because of the nature of the speech - not aimed at operational issues common to the company). These are 1) believing in yourself (connect the dots), 2) not compromising with mediocrity (don`t settle) and 3) the continuous thirst and pursuit of the dream by everyone (stay hungry, stay foolish). In his 15 minute speech, he manages to focus on these three key messages, repeating the central concept and relating the three stories, injecting an element of simplicity combined with originality in order to win over the audience with the content of the speech.

Referring finally to the degree of influence of the speech, I would say that it accomplishes much more with respect to the verbal part than with its audiovisual, as analyzed below.

Visual Persuasion

Appearance (+10)
10 Points. Because of the known character (art of authority) in combination with the characteristics of the speaker (relatively attractive).
Dress (Close to the audience's [Art of Liking], Professional [Art of Authority]) (+10)
10 Points. He combines successfully the art of authority (university robe) and the art of liking (everyone is dressed like him)
Body Position and Moves (+10)
10 Points. Erect and haughty attitude behind the podium.
Arms and Legs Position and Moves (+10)
0 Points. No help from his hands that seem awkward when they appear. Legs do not appear.
Continuous Contact with the audience (Does not read the speech) (+10)

2 points. Continuous reading of the speech with a few exceptions and almost total lack of eye contact with the audience.

Auditory Persuasion

Speed and Pace of Talking (+10)
10 Points. Good speed and pace of speech.
Volume (+10)
10 Points. Satisfactory volume of the speech
Exploitation of Pauses (+10)
3 Points. Incomplete use of pauses.
Articulation (+10)
5 Points. Satisfactory articulation with a few mistakes but it does not help as much as it could.
Intonation (+10)
6 points. Satisfactory intonation with a few mistakes but it does not help as much it could.

Verbal Persuasion

Morality:

Consistency with what he said in the Past (Art of Consistency) (+10)
10 Points. There seem to be no contradictions while he seems to be consistent in his beliefs.

Recognition of errors and correction (+10)

10 Points. Recognizes the mistakes of the past commenting on them in conjunction with proposals to emulate or avoid.

Speech Content and Main Message:

Confirms Goals, Vision and Mission of the Organization (+10)

10 Points. Absolute commitment to the goals and vision of the audience.

Comparison of successes and failures for the benefit of the speaker and the company (Art of Comparison) (+10)

10 Points. Continuous comparison of the successes and failures of the speaker.

Relevance of Speech to its Topics and Goals (+10)

10 Points. Absolute connection between the topics and objectives of the speech.

The Audience is at the center of the Speech ("What could I earn?" Promises for better working conditions, future-benefits for the company, references to the, 'employees', 'partners' and 'stakeholders' [Art of Reciprocation]) (+10)

10 Points. The audience is at the center of the speech and its messages.

Initiative for change (+10)

10 Points. Initiative to change the entrenched perception of what the speaker considers important.

Call for Action (+10)

10 Points. Call for action and encouragement for a particular direction.

Simplicity of speech (+10)

10 Points. Simplicity of speech.

Originality of phrases and words used (Art of Scarcity) (+10)

10 Points. Originality of phrases and words used (Stay Hungry, stay foolish).

Repetition of the main message (+10)

10 Points. Continuous repetition of the main messages.

Transmission and Retention of the Message:

Babbling (thanking too much etc.) (-10)

0 Points. Absolute lack of babbling.

Shortness of speech (+10)

10 Points. Ideal Length of Speech.

Theatricality (Too much, reasonable) (-10, +10)

0 Points. Lack of Theatricality.

Compliments to the Audience (Art of Liking, Art of Reciprocation) (+10)

10 Points. Indirect compliments for the Foundation. Compliments for people who he does not know may seem excessive.

Failed Jokes (-10)

0 Points. Lack of failed jokes.

Successful Jokes (Art of Scarcity) (+10)

2 points. Very modest but successful jokes.

Self-sarcasm (+10)

2 points. Very few attempts at self-sarcasm ("How can you get fired from your own company?")

Use of Stories and Examples (Social Proof, Art of Scarcity) (+10)

10 Points. One of the most successful examples of using stories and examples in speeches in general.

Verbal Content and Linking Phrases:

Statistics (too many, reasonable [Art of Authority]) (-10,+10)

0 Points. Lack of Statistics.

Logical Verbal Links ('but', 'because', 'also', 'and', 'so') (+10)

8 Points. 'But' (14 times), 'because' (4 times), 'also' (0 times), 'and' (69 times), 'so' (17 times).

Verbal Sequencing Links ('firstly', 'secondly', 'in addition', 'finally') (+10)

10 Points. Use of verbal sequencing connectors for the three key messages-stories.

Verbal Links of Probability ('maybe', 'possibly', 'probably') (+10)

0 Points. Lack of Verbal Links of Probability.

Emphatic Verbal Links ('in reality', 'certainly', 'definitely') (+10)

5 Points. 'Certainly' (2 times)

Citing Verbal Links ('according to', 'X said') (+10)

0 Points. Lack of citing verbal links.

Emotional Verbal Links ('I', 'we', 'between us') (+10)

10 Points. Use of 'I' (86 times) and 'we' (10 times).

<u>Overall Degree of Speaker's Influence:</u> = [- 40 (min.), 340 (max.)]

243 Points

Rex Tillerson (Exxon Mobil)

Rex Tillerson's speech has approximately the same length as the speech of Jobs, it took place in an international oil conference and was addressed to key stakeholders and employees of the company.

It succeeds in presenting the data and future capabilities of the organization, encouraging indirectly its staff as regards the potential of the company and the industry in general.

Finally, concerning the degree of influence of the speech, I would say that it achieves more as far as the verbal part is concerned than the audiovisual, as discussed below, but in any case it cannot be characterized as a good speech.

Visual Persuasion

Appearance (+10)

10 Points. Because of the known character (art of authority) in combination with the characteristics of the speaker (relatively attractive).

Dress (Close to the audience's [Art of Liking], Professional [Art of Authority]) (+10)

10 Points. He combines successfully the art of authority (business suit) and the art of liking (everyone is dressed like him)

Body Position and Moves (+10)

10 Points. Erect and haughty attitude behind the podium.

Arms and Legs Position and Moves (+10)

0 Points. No help from his hands. Legs do not appear.

Continuous Contact with the audience (Does not read the speech) (+10)

4 points. Continuous reading of the speech with a few exceptions and almost total lack of eye contact with the audience.

Auditory Persuasion

Speed and Pace of Talking (+10)

10 Points. Good speed and pace of speech.

Volume (+10)

10 Points. Satisfactory volume of the speech

Exploitation of Pauses (+10)

4 Points. Incomplete use of pauses.

Articulation (+10)

2 Points. Problematic articulation with a lot of mistakes.

Intonation (+10)

7 points. Satisfactory intonation with a few mistakes but it does not help as much it could.

Verbal Persuasion

<u>Morality:</u>

Consistency with what was said in the Past (Art of Consistency) (+10)
0 Points. There are no indications.
Recognition of errors and correction (+10)
0 Points. There is no recognition of mistakes in the past.

<u>Speech Content and Main Message:</u>

Confirms Goals, Vision and Mission of the Organization (+10)
10 Points. Absolute commitment to the goals and vision of the audience.
Comparison of successes and failures for the benefit of the speaker and the company (Art of Comparison) (+10)
0 Points. No comparisons.
Relevance of Speech to its Topics and Goals (+10)
10 Points. Absolute connection between the topics and objectives of the speech.
The Audience is at the center of the Speech ("What could I earn?" Promises for better working conditions, future-benefits for the company, references to the, 'employees', 'partners' and 'stakeholders' [Art of Reciprocation]) (+10)
10 Points. The audience is at the center of the speech and its messages.

Initiative for change (+10)

0 Points. No Initiative for change.

Call for Action (+10)

0 Points. No Call for action.

Simplicity of speech (+10)

8 Points. Simplicity of speech with a few exceptions that are justified due to the purpose and the audience of the speech.

Originality of phrases and words used (Art of Scarcity) (+10)

0 Points. There is no originality in the phrases and words used.

Repetition of the main message (+10)

0 Points. No repetition of the main messages.

Transmission and Retention of the Message:

Babbling (thanking too much etc.) (-10)

-2 Points. Tolerable babbling.

Shortness of speech (+10)

10 Points. Ideal Length of Speech.

Theatricality (Too much, reasonable) (-10, +10)

0 Points. Lack of Theatricality.

Compliments to the Audience (Art of Liking, Art of Reciprocation) (+10)

10 Points. Indirect compliments.

Failed Jokes (-10)

0 Points. Lack of failed jokes.

Successful Jokes (Art of Scarcity) (+10)

0 points. No jokes attempted.
Self-sarcasm (+10)
0 points. No attempts at self-sarcasm.
Use of Stories and Examples (Social Proof, Art of Scarcity) (+10)
0 Points. No stories used.

Verbal Content and Linking Phrases:

Statistics (too many, reasonable [Art of Authority]) (-10,+10)
4 Points. Quite a lot but tolerable use of Statistics.
Logical Verbal Links ('but', 'because', 'also', 'and', 'so') (+10)
6 Points. 'But' (2 times), 'because' (1 time), 'also' (7 times), 'and' (143 times), 'so' (4 times).
Verbal Sequencing Links ('firstly', 'secondly', 'in addition', 'finally') (+10)
8 Points. Use of verbal connections but not very clearly.
Verbal Links of Probability ('maybe', 'possibly', 'probably') (+10)
0 Points. Lack of Verbal Links of Probability.
Emphatic Verbal Links ('in reality', 'certainly', 'definitely') (+10)
0 Points. Lack of Emphatic Verbal Links.
Citing Verbal Links ('according to', 'X said') (+10)
7 Points. 1 citation to official records.
Emotional Verbal Links ('I', 'we', 'between us') (+10)
10 Points. Use of 'I' (1 time) and 'we' (37 times).

<u>Overall Degree of Speaker's Influence:</u> = [- 40 (min.), 340 (max.)]

136 Points

Larry Page (Google)

The speech given by Larry Page is addressed mainly to graduate students in their graduation ceremony (prospective or existing employees) and it succeeds in delivering simple messages to the audience (regarding HRM). It mainly tries to encourage the audience and less to reward it (which makes sense because of the nature of the speech – it is not addressed for operational issues common to the company). The messages conveyed are (very similar to Jobs' speech) self-confidence and the constant thirst and pursuit of dreams.

In his speech, which is similar in length to previous ones, he tries to focus on these messages using personal stories in order to arouse emotions, but he gives the impression that he is pushing a little more than he should towards this direction.

As regards the degree of influence of the speech, I would say that it achieves more as far as the verbal is concerned than the audiovisual part, as analyzed below.

Visual Persuasion

Appearance (+10)

8 Points. Because of the known character (art of authority) in combination with the characteristics of the speaker (relatively attractive but with an eye problem).

Dress (Close to the audience's [Art of Liking], Professional [Art of Authority]) (+10)

10 Points. He combines successfully the art of authority (university robe) and the art of liking (everyone is dressed like him)

Body Position and Moves (+10)

7 Points. Erect position behind the podium but with several awkward moves.

Arms and Legs Position and Moves (+10)

0 Points. No help from his hands. Legs do not appear.

Continuous Contact with the audience (Does not read the speech) (+10)

6 points. Continuous reading of the speech with several exceptions.

Auditory Persuasion

Speed and Pace of Talking (+10)

10 Points. Good speed and pace of speech.

Volume (+10)

10 Points. Satisfactory volume of the speech

Exploitation of Pauses (+10)

2 Points. Incomplete use of pauses.

Articulation (+10)

2 Points. Unsatisfactory articulation with several mistakes.

Intonation (+10)

4 points. Unsatisfactory intonation with a few mistakes but it does not help as much it could.

Verbal Persuasion

Morality:

Consistency with what he said in the Past (Art of Consistency) (+10)

10 Points. There seem to be no contradictions while he seems to be consistent in his beliefs.

Recognition of errors and correction (+10)

0 Points. He does not recognize mistakes of the past.

Speech Content and Main Message:

Confirms Goals, Vision and Mission of the Organization (+10)

8 Points. Commitment to the goals and visions of the audience.

Comparison of successes and failures for the benefit of the speaker and the company (Art of Comparison) (+10)

8 Points. Comparison of the successes of the speaker.

Relevance of Speech to its Topics and Goals (+10)

10 Points. Absolute connection between the topics and objectives of the speech.

The Audience is at the center of the Speech ("What could I earn?" Promises for better working conditions, future-benefits for the company, references to the, 'employees', 'partners' and 'stakeholders' [Art of Reciprocation]) (+10)

8 Points. The audience is at the center of the speech.

Initiative for change (+10)

10 Points. Initiative for changing the entrenched perception of what the speaker considers important.

Call for Action (+10)

10 Points. Call for action and encouragement for a particular direction.

Simplicity of speech (+10)

10 Points. Simplicity of speech.

Originality of phrases and words used (Art of Scarcity) (+10)

0 Points. No originality of phrases and words used.

Repetition of the main message (+10)

0 Points. No repetition nor main messages.

Transmission and Retention of the Message:

Babbling (thanking too much etc.) (-10)

0 Points. Absolute lack of babbling.

Shortness of speech (+10)

10 Points. Ideal Length of Speech.

Theatricality (Too much, reasonable) (-10, +10)

0 Points. Lack of Theatricality.

Compliments to the Audience (Art of Liking, Art of Reciprocation) (+10)

8 Points. Indirect and controversial compliments for the Foundation. Compliments for people who he does not know may seem excessive.

Failed Jokes (-10)

-8 Points. A lot of failed jokes.

Successful Jokes (Art of Scarcity) (+10)

4 points. A few successful jokes.

Self-sarcasm (+10)

2 points. Very few attempts at self-sarcasm.

Use of Stories and Examples (Social Proof, Art of Scarcity) (+10)

6 Points. Use of stories, though not always successfully.

Verbal Content and Linking Phrases:

Statistics (too many, reasonable [Art of Authority]) (-10,+10)

0 Points. Lack of Statistics.

Logical Verbal Links ('but', 'because', 'also', 'and', 'so') (+10)

7 Points. 'But' (7 times), 'because' (3 times), 'also' (0 times), 'and' (62 times), 'so' (10 times).

Verbal Sequencing Links ('firstly', 'secondly', 'in addition', 'finally') (+10)

2 Points. Use of verbal sequencing connectors but not successfully.

Verbal Links of Probability ('maybe', 'possibly', 'probably') (+10)

7 Points. 'Maybe' (1 time), 'probably' (2 times).

Emphatic Verbal Links ('in reality', 'certainly', 'definitely') (+10)

0 Points. Lack of emphatic verbal links.

Citing Verbal Links ('according to', 'X said') (+10)

10 Points. References to his father and his supervisor.

Emotional Verbal Links ('I', 'we', 'between us') (+10)

10 Points. Use of 'I' (46 times) and 'we' (21 times).

Overall Degree of Speaker's Influence: = [- 40 (min.), 340 (max.)]

195 Points

Bill Gates (Microsoft)

The speech given by Bill Gates is shorter than the previous three by a quarter, it was made for a company conference and was addressed to the employees of the company (specifically of the Gates Foundation).

It succeeds in presenting the data and the future potential of the Foundation and its employees.

Finally, as far as it concerns the degree of influence of the speech, I would say that it manages equally between verbal and audiovisual persuasion.

Visual Persuasion

Appearance (+10)
7 Points. Because of the known character (art of authority) but in combination with the characteristics of the speaker (relatively unattractive).
Dress (Close to the audience's [Art of Liking], Professional [Art of Authority]) (+10)
10 Points. He combines successfully the art of authority (business suit) and the art of liking (everyone is dressed like him)
Body Position and Moves (+10)
7 Points. Erect but not haughty attitude behind the podium.
Arms and Legs Position and Moves (+10)

2 Points. Little help from his hands. Legs do not appear. Continuous Contact with the audience (Does not read the speech) (+10)

6 points. Continuous reading of the speech with several exceptions.

Auditory Persuasion

Speed and Pace of Talking (+10)

10 Points. Good speed and pace of speech.

Volume (+10)

7 Points. Unsatisfactory volume of the speech

Exploitation of Pauses (+10)

8 Points. Good use of pauses.

Articulation (+10)

2 Points. Problematic articulation with a lot of mistakes.

Intonation (+10)

7 points. Satisfactory intonation with a few mistakes but it does not help as much it could.

Verbal Persuasion

Morality:

Consistency with what he said in the Past (Art of Consistency) (+10)

0 Points. There are no indications.

Recognition of errors and correction (+10)

0 Points. There is no recognition of mistakes of the past.

Speech Content and Main Message:

Confirms Goals, Vision and Mission of the Organization (+10)

10 Points. Absolute commitment to the goals and vision of the audience.

Comparison of successes and failures for the benefit of the speaker and the company (Art of Comparison) (+10)

0 Points. No comparisons.

Relevance of Speech to its Topics and Goals (+10)

10 Points. Absolute connection between the topics and objectives of the speech.

The Audience is at the center of the Speech ("What could I earn?" Promises for better working conditions, future-benefits for the company, references to the, 'employees', 'partners' and 'stakeholders' [Art of Reciprocation]) (+10)

8 Points. The audience is at the center of the speech and its messages.

Initiative for change (+10)

0 Points. No Initiative for change.

Call for Action (+10)

3 Points. Indirect call for action.

Simplicity of speech (+10)

9 Points. Simplicity of speech with a few exceptions that are justified due to the purpose and the audience of the speech.

Originality of phrases and words used (Art of Scarcity) (+10)

0 Points. There is no originality in the phrases and words used.

Repetition of the main message (+10)

0 Points. No repetition of the main messages.

Transmission and Retention of the Message:

Babbling (thanking too much etc.) (-10)

0 Points. No babbling.

Shortness of speech (+10)

10 Points. Ideal Length of Speech.

Theatricality (Too much, reasonable) (-10, +10)

0 Points. Lack of Theatricality.

Compliments to the Audience (Art of Liking, Art of Reciprocation) (+10)

10 Points. Indirect compliments.

Failed Jokes (-10)

0 Points. Lack of failed jokes.

Successful Jokes (Art of Scarcity) (+10)

0 points. No jokes attempted.

Self-sarcasm (+10)

0 points. No attempts at self-sarcasm.

Use of Stories and Examples (Social Proof, Art of Scarcity) (+10)

6 Points. Not for the main message.

Verbal Content and Linking Phrases:

Statistics (too many, reasonable [Art of Authority]) (-10,+10)
10 Points. Reasonable use of Statistics.
Logical Verbal Links ('but', 'because', 'also', 'and', 'so') (+10)
6 Points. 'But' (6 times), 'because' (4 times), 'also' (0 times), 'and' (53 times), 'so' (16 times).
Verbal Sequencing Links ('firstly', 'secondly', 'in addition', 'finally') (+10)
8 Points. Use of verbal connectors but not very clearly.
Verbal Links of Probability ('maybe', 'possibly', 'probably') (+10)
7 Points. Use of 'maybe' (1 time), 'probably' (1 time).
Emphatic Verbal Links ('in reality', 'certainly', 'definitely') (+10)
0 Points. Lack of Emphatic Verbal Links.
Citing Verbal Links ('according to', 'X said') (+10)
0 Points. Lack of citing verbal links.
Emotional Verbal Links ('I', 'we', 'between us') (+10)
10 Points. Use of 'I' (9 times) and 'we' (25 times).

Overall Degree of Speaker's Influence: = [- 40 (min.), 340 (max.)]

174 Points

Warren Buffett (Berkshire Hathaway)

The speech (speech for the audiovisual judgment of the speaker - letter for the verbal) of Warren Buffett is identical in size to the first three, has to do with the progress of the company and is addressed to shareholders and employees of the company.

It succeeds in presenting the data and future capabilities of the organization, encouraging the staff as to the potential of the company and the industry in general, but also rewarding it with compliments directly made for them (it was a very good move to appoint X there etc.).

Finally, as far as the degree of influence of the speech is concerned, I would say that it achieves less with respect to the verbal part compared to the audio visual one (mainly due to the nature of the letter analyzed for the verbal part), as discussed below, and in any case he is characterized as a good speaker.

Visual Persuasion

Appearance (+10)
8 Points. Because of the known character (art of authority) but in combination with the characteristics of the speaker (relatively unattractive).

Dress (Close to the audience's [Art of Liking], Professional [Art of Authority]) (+10)

10 Points. He combines successfully the art of authority (business suit) and the art of liking (everyone is dressed like him)

Body Position and Moves (+10)

10 Points. Erect and haughty attitude in front of the podium.

Arms and Legs Position and Moves (+10)

10 Points. A lot of help from his hands. Legs appear steady.

Continuous Contact with the audience (Does not read the speech) (+10)

10 points. Continuous Contact with the audience (Does not read the speech).

Auditory Persuasion

Speed and Pace of Talking (+10)

10 Points. Good speed and pace of speech.

Volume (+10)

10 Points. Good volume of the speech

Exploitation of Pauses (+10)

10 Points. Good use of pauses.

Articulation (+10)

7 Points. Satisfactory articulation.

Intonation (+10)

8 points. Satisfactory intonation.

Verbal Persuasion

Consistency with what he said in the Past (Art of Consistency) (+10)
10 Points. Consistency with what he has said.
Recognition of errors and correction (+10)
5 Points. Recognition of mistakes that could take place but not of the past.

Speech Content and Main Message:

Confirms Goals, Vision and Mission of the Organization (+10)
10 Points. Absolute commitment to the goals and visions of the audience.
Comparison of successes and failures for the benefit of the speaker and the company (Art of Comparison) (+10)
10 Points. Comparisons with possible failures.
Relevance of Speech to its Topics and Goals (+10)
10 Points. Absolute connection between the topics and objectives of the speech.
The Audience is at the center of the Speech ("What could I earn?" Promises for better working conditions, future-benefits for the company, references to the, 'employees', 'partners' and 'stakeholders' [Art of Reciprocation]) (+10)
10 Points. The audience is at the center of the speech and its messages.
Initiative for change (+10)

0 Points. No Initiative for change.
Call for Action (+10)
3 Points. Indirect call for action.
Simplicity of speech (+10)
8 Points. Simplicity of speech with a few exceptions that are justified due to the purpose and the audience of the speech.
Originality of phrases and words used (Art of Scarcity) (+10)
0 Points. There is no originality in the phrases and words used.
Repetition of the main message (+10)
0 Points. No repetition of the main messages.

Transmission and Retention of the Message:

Babbling (thanking too much etc.) (-10)
0 Points. No babbling.
Shortness of speech (+10)
10 Points. Ideal Length of Speech.
Theatricality (Too much, reasonable) (-10, +10)
0 Points. Lack of Theatricality.
Compliments to the Audience (Art of Liking, Art of Reciprocation) (+10)
10 Points. Indirect compliments.
Failed Jokes (-10)
0 Points. Lack of failed jokes.
Successful Jokes (Art of Scarcity) (+10)
0 points. No jokes attempted.
Self-sarcasm (+10)

0 points. No attempts at self-sarcasm.
Use of Stories and Examples (Social Proof, Art of Scarcity) (+10)
0 Points. Lack of stories.

Verbal Content and Linking Phrases:

Statistics (too many, reasonable [Art of Authority]) (-10,+10)
10 Points. Reasonable use of Statistics.
Logical Verbal Links ('but', 'because', 'also', 'and', 'so') (+10)
10 Points. 'But' (14 times), 'because' (2 times), 'also' (4 times), 'and' (53 times), 'so' (10 times).
Verbal Sequencing Links ('firstly', 'secondly', 'in addition', 'finally') (+10)
6 Points. Use of verbal connectors but not very clearly.
Verbal Links of Probability ('maybe', 'possibly', 'probably') (+10)
10 Points. Use of 'maybe' (4 times), 'probably' (1 time).
Emphatic Verbal Links ('in reality', 'certainly', 'definitely') (+10)
4 Points. 'Certainly' (1 time).
Citing Verbal Links ('according to', 'X said') (+10)
0 Points. Lack of citing verbal links.
Emotional Verbal Links ('I', 'we', 'between us') (+10)
10 Points. Use of 'I' (25 times) and 'we' (29 times).

Overall Degree of Speaker's Influence: = [- 40 (min.), 340 (max.)]

229 Points

Alex Gorsky (Johnson & Johnson)

The speech given by Alex Gorsky is the smallest in size out of all the ones analyzed and is addressed to the employees of the company.

It aims to encourage the employees by focusing on the potential of the company and their own achievements, but also attempts to reward them with direct compliments.

Finally, as far as the degree of influence of the speech is concerned, I would say that it is less effective with respect to the verbal part than the audio visual one (mainly because of his physical presence), as discussed below, and in any case he could be described as a good speaker.

Visual Persuasion

Appearance (+10)
10 Points. Because of the known character (art of authority) but in combination with the characteristics of the speaker (relatively handsome).
Dress (Close to the audience's [Art of Liking], Professional [Art of Authority]) (+10)

10 Points. He combines successfully the art of authority (business suit) and the art of liking (everyone is dressed like him)

Body Position and Moves (+10)

10 Points. Erect and haughty attitude in front of the podium.

Arms and Legs Position and Moves (+10)

10 Points. A lot of help from his hands. Legs appear steady.

Continuous Contact with the audience (Does not read the speech) (+10)

10 points. Continuous Contact with the audience (Does not read the speech).

Auditory Persuasion

Speed and Pace of Talking (+10)

10 Points. Good speed and pace of speech.

Volume (+10)

10 Points. Good volume of the speech

Exploitation of Pauses (+10)

10 Points. Good use of pauses.

Articulation (+10)

8 Points. Satisfactory articulation.

Intonation (+10)

8 points. Satisfactory intonation.

Verbal Persuasion

Morality:

Consistency with what he said in the Past (Art of Consistency) (+10)
0 Points. No indications.
Recognition of errors and correction (+10)
0 Points. No indication.

Speech Content and Main Message:

Confirms Goals, Vision and Mission of the Organization (+10)
10 Points. Absolute commitment to the goals and visions of the audience.
Comparison of successes and failures for the benefit of the speaker and the company (Art of Comparison) (+10)
0 Points. No Comparisons.
Relevance of Speech to its Topics and Goals (+10)
10 Points. Absolute connection between the topics and objectives of the speech.
The Audience is at the center of the Speech ("What could I earn?" Promises for better working conditions, future-benefits for the company, references to the, 'employees', 'partners' and 'stakeholders' [Art of Reciprocation]) (+10)
10 Points. The audience is at the center of the speech and its messages.
Initiative for change (+10)
0 Points. No Initiative for change.

Call for Action (+10)

10 Points. Direct call for action.

Simplicity of speech (+10)

10 Points. Simplicity of speech.

Originality of phrases and words used (Art of Scarcity) (+10)

0 Points. There is no originality in the phrases and words used.

Repetition of the main message (+10)

0 Points. No repetition of the main messages.

Transmission and Retention of the Message:

Babbling (thanking too much etc.) (-10)

0 Points. No babbling.

Shortness of speech (+10)

10 Points. Ideal Length of Speech.

Theatricality (Too much, reasonable) (-10, +10)

0 Points. Lack of Theatricality.

Compliments to the Audience (Art of Liking, Art of Reciprocation) (+10)

10 Points. Direct and Indirect compliments.

Failed Jokes (-10)

0 Points. Lack of failed jokes.

Successful Jokes (Art of Scarcity) (+10)

0 points. No jokes attempted.

Self-sarcasm (+10)

0 points. No attempts at self-sarcasm.

Use of Stories and Examples (Social Proof, Art of Scarcity) (+10)

0 Points. Lack of stories.

<u>Verbal Content and Linking Phrases:</u>

Statistics (too many, reasonable [Art of Authority]) (-10,+10)

0 Points. Lack of Statistics.

Logical Verbal Links ('but', 'because', 'also', 'and', 'so') (+10)

7 Points. 'But' (3 times), 'because' (0 times), 'also' (1 times), 'and' (16 times), 'so' (0 times).

Verbal Sequencing Links ('firstly', 'secondly', 'in addition', 'finally') (+10)

0 Points. Lack of Verbal Sequencing Links.

Verbal Links of Probability ('maybe', 'possibly', 'probably') (+10)

0 Points. Lack of Verbal Links of probability.

Emphatic Verbal Links ('in reality', 'certainly', 'definitely') (+10)

0 Points. Lack of Emphatic verbal links.

Citing Verbal Links ('according to', 'X said') (+10)

0 Points. Lack of citing verbal links.

Emotional Verbal Links ('I', 'we', 'between us') (+10)

10 Points. Use of 'I' (5 times) and 'we' (9 times).

<u>Overall Degree of Speaker's Influence:</u> = [- 40 (min.), 340 (max.)]

193 Points

John Stumpf (Wells Fargo)

The speech given by John Stumpf is about the same in size as the previous one and is addressed to shareholders and employees of the company.

It aims to encourage the employees by giving the potential of the company and their own achievements a special focus, but also attempts to reward them with direct compliments.

Finally, as far as the degree of influence of the speech is concerned, I would say that it is less effective with respect to the verbal part than the audio visual one, as discussed below, and in any case he could be described as a good speaker.

Visual Persuasion

Appearance (+10)

10 Points. Because of the known character (art of authority) in combination with the characteristics of the speaker (relatively attractive).

Dress (Close to the audience's [Art of Liking], Professional [Art of Authority]) (+10)

10 Points. He combines successfully the art of authority (business suit) and the art of liking (everyone is dressed like him)

Body Position and Moves (+10)

8 Points. Erect and relatively haughty attitude in front of the podium.

Arms and Legs Position and Moves (+10)

10 Points. A lot of help from his hands. Legs appear steady.

Continuous Contact with the audience (Does not read the speech) (+10)

10 points. Continuous Contact with the audience (Does not read the speech).

Auditory Persuasion

Speed and Pace of Talking (+10)

10 Points. Good speed and pace of speech.

Volume (+10)

10 Points. Good volume of the speech

Exploitation of Pauses (+10)

10 Points. Good use of pauses.

Articulation (+10)

7 Points. Satisfactory articulation.

Intonation (+10)

8 points. Satisfactory intonation.

Verbal Persuasion

<u>Morality:</u>

Consistency with what he said in the Past (Art of Consistency) (+10)
0 Points. No indications.
Recognition of errors and correction (+10)
0 Points. No indications.

<u>Speech Content and Main Message:</u>

Confirms Goals, Vision and Mission of the Organization (+10)
10 Points. Absolute commitment to the goals and vision of the audience.
Comparison of successes and failures for the benefit of the speaker and the company (Art of Comparison) (+10)
0 Points. No comparisons.
Relevance of Speech to its Topics and Goals (+10)
10 Points. Absolute connection between the topics and objectives of the speech.
The Audience is at the center of the Speech ("What could I earn?" Promises for better working conditions, future-benefits for the company, references to the, 'employees', 'partners' and 'stakeholders' [Art of Reciprocation]) (+10)
10 Points. The audience is at the center of the speech and its messages.
Initiative for change (+10)
0 Points. No Initiative for change.
Call for Action (+10)
0 Points. No call for action.

Simplicity of speech (+10)

8 Points. Simplicity of speech with a few exceptions that are justified due to the purpose and the audience of the speech.

Originality of phrases and words used (Art of Scarcity) (+10)

0 Points. There is no originality in the phrases and words used.

Repetition of the main message (+10)

0 Points. No repetition of the main messages.

Transmission and Retention of the Message:

Babbling (thanking too much etc.) (-10)

0 Points. No babbling.

Shortness of speech (+10)

10 Points. Ideal Length of Speech.

Theatricality (Too much, reasonable) (-10, +10)

0 Points. Lack of Theatricality.

Compliments to the Audience (Art of Liking, Art of Reciprocation) (+10)

10 Points. Direct and indirect compliments.

Failed Jokes (-10)

0 Points. Lack of failed jokes.

Successful Jokes (Art of Scarcity) (+10)

0 points. No jokes attempted.

Self-sarcasm (+10)

0 points. No attempts at self-sarcasm.

Use of Stories and Examples (Social Proof, Art of Scarcity) (+10)

0 Points. Lack of stories.

<u>Verbal Content and Linking Phrases:</u>

Statistics (too many, reasonable [Art of Authority]) (-10,+10)
6 Points. Use of Statistics (a little more than reasonable).
Logical Verbal Links ('but', 'because', 'also', 'and', 'so') (+10)
4 Points. 'But' (0 times), 'because' (0 times), 'also' (2 times), 'and' (11 times), 'so' (0 times).
Verbal Sequencing Links ('firstly', 'secondly', 'in addition', 'finally') (+10)
0 Points. No use.
Verbal Links of Probability ('maybe', 'possibly', 'probably') (+10)
0 Points. No use.
Emphatic Verbal Links ('in reality', 'certainly', 'definitely') (+10)
0 Points. No use.
Citing Verbal Links ('according to', 'X said') (+10)
0 Points. Lack of citing verbal links.
Emotional Verbal Links ('I', 'we', 'between us') (+10)
10 Points. Use of 'I' (1 time) and 'we' (9 times).

<u>Overall Degree of Speaker's Influence:</u> = [- 40 (min.), 340 (max.)]

191 Points

Jeff Immelt (General Electric)

The speech given by Jeff Immelt is the longest out of all those I have analyzed, nearly double the size of the first three and aimed primarily at employees (current and future) of the company.

It aims to encourage the employees by focusing on the potential of the company and their own achievements and future, but also attempts to reward them with direct compliments.

Finally, as far as the degree of influence of the speech is concerned, I would say that it is rather balanced with respect to the verbal part and the audio visual one, as discussed below, and in any case he could be described as a very good speaker.

Visual Persuasion

Appearance (+10)

8 Points. Because of the known character (art of authority) but in combination with the characteristics of the speaker (relatively unattractive).

Dress (Close to the audience's [Art of Liking], Professional [Art of Authority]) (+10)

10 Points. He combines successfully the art of authority (business suit) and the art of liking (everyone is dressed like him)

Body Position and Moves (+10)

8 Points. Erect and relatively haughty attitude in front of the podium.

Arms and Legs Position and Moves (+10)

8 Points. Some help from his hands. Legs appear steady.

Continuous Contact with the audience (Does not read the speech) (+10)

10 points. Continuous Contact with the audience (Does not read the speech).

Auditory Persuasion

Speed and Pace of Talking (+10)

10 Points. Good speed and pace of speech.

Volume (+10)

10 Points. Good volume of the speech

Exploitation of Pauses (+10)

10 Points. Good use of pauses.

Articulation (+10)

8 Points. Satisfactory articulation.

Intonation (+10)

8 points. Satisfactory intonation.

Verbal Persuasion

<u>Morality:</u>

Consistency with what he said in the Past (Art of Consistency) (+10)
10 Points. Consistency with what he has said.
Recognition of errors and correction (+10)
10 Points. Recognition of mistakes.

<u>Speech Content and Main Message:</u>

Confirms Goals, Vision and Mission of the Organization (+10)
10 Points. Absolute commitment to the goals and visions of the audience.
Comparison of successes and failures for the benefit of the speaker and the company (Art of Comparison) (+10)
10 Points. Comparisons with possible failures.
Relevance of Speech to its Topics and Goals (+10)
10 Points. Absolute connection between the topics and objectives of the speech.
The Audience is at the center of the Speech ("What could I earn?" Promises for better working conditions, future-benefits for the company, references to the, 'employees', 'partners' and 'stakeholders' [Art of Reciprocation]) (+10)
10 Points. The audience is at the center of the speech and its messages.
Initiative for change (+10)

10 Points. Change is the central meaning.
Call for Action (+10)
10 Points. Direct call for action.
Simplicity of speech (+10)
8 Points. Simplicity of speech with a few exceptions that are justified due to the purpose and the audience of the speech.
Originality of phrases and words used (Art of Scarcity) (+10)
0 Points. There is no originality in the phrases and words used.
Repetition of the main message (+10)
0 Points. No repetition of the main messages.

Transmission and Retention of the Message:

Babbling (thanking too much etc.) (-10)
0 Points. No babbling.
Shortness of speech (+10)
6 Points. Relatively Short.
Theatricality (Too much, reasonable) (-10, +10)
0 Points. Lack of Theatricality.
Compliments to the Audience (Art of Liking, Art of Reciprocation) (+10)
8 Points. Several compliments.
Failed Jokes (-10)
0 Points. Lack of failed jokes.
Successful Jokes (Art of Scarcity) (+10)
0 points. No jokes attempted.

Self-sarcasm (+10)

0 points. No attempts at self-sarcasm.

Use of Stories and Examples (Social Proof, Art of Scarcity) (+10)

0 Points. Lack of stories.

Verbal Content and Linking Phrases:

Statistics (too many, reasonable [Art of Authority]) (-10,+10)

10 Points. Reasonable use of Statistics.

Logical Verbal Links ('but', 'because', 'also', 'and', 'so') (+10)

10 Points. 'But' (19 times), 'because' (10 times), 'also' (8 times), 'and' (53 times), 'so' (14 times).

Verbal Sequencing Links ('firstly', 'secondly', 'in addition', 'finally') (+10)

10 Points. Use of clear verbal sequencing connectors.

Verbal Links of Probability ('maybe', 'possibly', 'probably') (+10)

3 Points. Use of 'probably' (1 time).

Emphatic Verbal Links ('in reality', 'certainly', 'definitely') (+10)

3 Points. 'Certainly' (1 time).

Citing Verbal Links ('according to', 'X said') (+10)

0 Points. Lack of citing verbal links.

Emotional Verbal Links ('I', 'we', 'between us') (+10)

10 Points. Use of 'I' (23 times) and 'we' (106 times).

Overall Degree of Speaker's Influence: = [- 40 (min.), 340 (max.)]

230 Points

Severin Schwan (Roche Holding)

The speech of Severin Schwan is about the same in size with the first three and was given at the annual conference of the company. It is aimed primarily at employees and shareholders of the company.

Its aims are to encourage the employees by highlighting the company's potential and their own achievements now and in the future, but also attempts to reward them with direct compliments.

Finally, as far as the degree of influence of the speech is concerned, I would say that the verbal part is better than the audio visual one, as discussed below, and in any case he has to be described as a relatively poor speaker.

Visual Persuasion

Appearance (+10)
8 Points. Because of the known character (art of authority) but in combination with the characteristics of the speaker (relatively unattractive).
Dress (Close to the audience's [Art of Liking], Professional [Art of Authority]) (+10)

8 Points. He combines poorly the art of authority (business suit - no tie) and the art of liking (everyone is dressed like him)

Body Position and Moves (+10)

6 Points. Erect but not haughty attitude in front of the podium.

Arms and Legs Position and Moves (+10)

6 Points. Some help from his hands. Legs appear steady.

Continuous Contact with the audience (Does not read the speech) (+10)

10 points. Continuous Contact with the audience (Does not read the speech).

Auditory Persuasion

Speed and Pace of Talking (+10)

10 Points. Good speed and pace of speech.

Volume (+10)

10 Points. Good volume of the speech

Exploitation of Pauses (+10)

10 Points. Good use of pauses.

Articulation (+10)

6 Points. Satisfactory articulation.

Intonation (+10)

8 points. Satisfactory intonation.

Verbal Persuasion

<u>Morality:</u>

Consistency with what he said in the Past (Art of Consistency) (+10)
0 Points. No indications.
Recognition of errors and correction (+10)
0 Points. No indications.

<u>Speech Content and Main Message:</u>

Confirms Goals, Vision and Mission of the Organization (+10)
10 Points. Absolute commitment to the goals and vision of the audience.
Comparison of successes and failures for the benefit of the speaker and the company (Art of Comparison) (+10)
0 Points. No Comparisons.
Relevance of Speech to its Topics and Goals (+10)
10 Points. Absolute connection between the topics and objectives of the speech.
The Audience is at the center of the Speech ("What could I earn?" Promises for better working conditions, future-benefits for the company, references to the, 'employees', 'partners' and 'stakeholders' [Art of Reciprocation]) (+10)
10 Points. The audience is at the center of the speech and its messages.

Initiative for change (+10)

0 Points. No Initiative for change.

Call for Action (+10)

0 Points. No call for action.

Simplicity of speech (+10)

8 Points. Simplicity of the speech with a few exceptions that are justified due to the purpose and the audience of the speech.

Originality of phrases and words used (Art of Scarcity) (+10)

0 Points. There is no originality in the phrases and words used.

Repetition of the main message (+10)

0 Points. No repetition of the main messages.

Transmission and Retention of the Message:

Babbling (thanking too much etc.) (-10)

0 Points. No babbling.

Shortness of speech (+10)

10 Points. Ideal Length of Speech.

Theatricality (Too much, reasonable) (-10, +10)

0 Points. Lack of Theatricality.

Compliments to the Audience (Art of Liking, Art of Reciprocation) (+10)

8 Points. Direct and Indirect compliments.

Failed Jokes (-10)

0 Points. Lack of failed jokes.

Successful Jokes (Art of Scarcity) (+10)

0 points. No jokes attempted.
Self-sarcasm (+10)
0 points. No attempts at self-sarcasm.
Use of Stories and Examples (Social Proof, Art of Scarcity) (+10)
0 Points. Lack of stories.

Verbal Content and Linking Phrases:

Statistics (too many, reasonable [Art of Authority]) (-10,+10)
-2 Points. Excessive use of Statistics.
Logical Verbal Links ('but', 'because', 'also', 'and', 'so') (+10)
9 Points. 'But' (3 times), 'because' (1 times), 'also' (7 times), 'and' (66 times), 'so' (11 times).
Verbal Sequencing Links ('firstly', 'secondly', 'in addition', 'finally') (+10)
8 Points. Use of verbal connections but not very clearly.
Verbal Links of Probability ('maybe', 'possibly', 'probably') (+10)
5 Points. Use of 'probably' (2 times).
Emphatic Verbal Links ('in reality', 'certainly', 'definitely') (+10)
0 Points. No use.
Citing Verbal Links ('according to', 'X said') (+10)
0 Points. Lack of citing verbal links.
Emotional Verbal Links ('I', 'we', 'between us') (+10)
10 Points. Use of 'I' (16 times) and 'we' (37 times).

Overall Degree of Speaker's Influence: = [- 40 (min.), 340 (max.)]

167 Points

Doug Mcmillon (Wal-Mart)

The speech given by Doug Mcmillon is equal in size to the first three, and was presented at the meeting of company shareholders and is mainly aimed at employees, partners and shareholders of the company (i.e. probably the same person because of company policy to give shares to employees as a way optimizing work performance).

It aims to encourage employees by focusing on the potential of the company and their own achievements now and in the future, but also attempts to reward them with direct compliments about their capabilities and future prospects as employees and stakeholders, because of the company's policy to award stocks to its employees.

Finally, as far as the degree of influence of the speech is concerned, I would say that it is rather balanced with respect to the verbal part and the audio visual one, as discussed below, and in any case he could be described as a very good speaker.

Visual Persuasion

Appearance (+10)

10 Points. Because of the known character (art of authority) but in combination with the characteristics of the speaker (relatively attractive).

Dress (Close to the audience's [Art of Liking], Professional [Art of Authority]) (+10)

10 Points. He combines successfully the art of authority (business suit) and the art of liking (everyone is dressed like him)

Body Position and Moves (+10)

10 Points. Erect and haughty attitude in front of the podium.

Arms and Legs Position and Moves (+10)

0 Points. No help from his hands. Legs appear steady.

Continuous Contact with the audience (Does not read the speech) (+10)

10 points. Continuous Contact with the audience (Does not read the speech).

Auditory Persuasion

Speed and Pace of Talking (+10)

10 Points. Good speed and pace of speech.

Volume (+10)

10 Points. Good volume of the speech

Exploitation of Pauses (+10)

10 Points. Good use of pauses.

Articulation (+10)

8 Points. Satisfactory articulation.

Intonation (+10)
8 points. Satisfactory intonation.

Verbal Persuasion

<u>Morality:</u>

Consistency with what he said in the Past (Art of Consistency) (+10)
0 Points. No indication.
Recognition of errors and correction (+10)
0 Points. No indication.

<u>Speech Content and Main Message:</u>

Confirm Goals, Vision and Mission of the Organization (+10)
10 Points. Absolute commitment to the goals and visions of the audience.
Comparison of successes and failures for the benefit of the speaker and the company (Art of Comparison) (+10)
0 Points. No Comparisons.
Relevance of Speech to its Topics and Goals (+10)
10 Points. Absolute connection between the topics and objectives of the speech.
The Audience is at the center of the Speech ("What could I earn?" Promises for better working conditions, future-

benefits for the company, references to the, 'employees', 'partners' and 'stakeholders' [Art of Reciprocation]) (+10)

10 Points. The audience is at the center of the speech and its messages.

Initiative for change (+10)

0 Points. No Initiative for change.

Call for Action (+10)

0 Points. No call for action.

Simplicity of speech (+10)

10 Points. Simplicity of speech.

Originality of phrases and words used (Art of Scarcity) (+10)

0 Points. There is no originality in the phrases and words used.

Repetition of the main message (+10)

0 Points. No repetition of the main messages.

Transmission and Retention of the Message:

Babbling (thanking too much etc.) (-10)

0 Points. No babbling.

Shortness of speech (+10)

10 Points. Ideal Length of Speech.

Theatricality (Too much, reasonable) (-10, +10)

0 Points. Lack of Theatricality.

Compliments to the Audience (Art of Liking, Art of Reciprocation) (+10)

10 Points. Direct and Indirect compliments.

Failed Jokes (-10)

0 Points. Lack of failed jokes.
Successful Jokes (Art of Scarcity) (+10)
0 points. No jokes attempted.
Self-sarcasm (+10)
0 points. No attempts at self-sarcasm.
Use of Stories and Examples (Social Proof, Art of Scarcity) (+10)
7 Points. Use of stories.

Verbal Content and Linking Phrases:

Statistics (too many, reasonable [Art of Authority]) (-10,+10)
10 Points. Reasonable use of Statistics.
Logical Verbal Links ('but', 'because', 'also', 'and', 'so') (+10)
10 Points. 'But' (7 times), 'because' (2 times), 'also' (8 times), 'and' (103 times), 'so' (17 times).
Verbal Sequencing Links ('firstly', 'secondly', 'in addition', 'finally') (+10)
10 Points. Good use of verbal connectors.
Verbal Links of Probability ('maybe', 'possibly', 'probably') (+10)
10 Points. Use of 'maybe' (3 times), 'probably' (3 times).
Emphatic Verbal Links ('in reality', 'certainly', 'definitely') (+10)
0 Points. No use.
Citing Verbal Links ('according to', 'X said') (+10)
5 Points. 1 citation.

Emotional Verbal Links ('I', 'we', 'between us') (+10)
10 Points. Use of 'I' (20 times) and 'we' (59 times).

Overall Degree of Speaker's Influence: = [- 40 (min.), 340 (max.)]

208 Points

Conclusions

In this book I have tried to highlight the importance of the influence of corporate speeches on employees, how they become effective and what their aims are. In order to analyze the effectiveness of three different forms of persuasion: visual, auditory and verbal, I created the 'Overall Degree of Speaker's Influence', taking into account several criteria based on the existing literature.

According therefore to the overall degree of a speaker's influence, the first of the 10 is the former CEO of Apple, Steve Jobs with 243 points, second is Jeff Immelt with 230 points, third comes Warren Buffett with 229 points and fourth Doug McMillon with 208 points. Below 200 points we find Larry Page with 195 points, Alex Gorsky with 193, John Stumpf with 191, Bill Gates with 174, Severin Schwan with 167 and finally Rex Tillerson with 136 points. Therefore, based on these results, we could conclude that from 0 to 150 points we have a speaker with little influence on the audience, from 150-200, a speaker with moderate influence, from 200-250 an influential speaker and from 250-340 points an extremely influential speaker, a real orator.

But beyond the capacity to influence in each of the above, the importance of this treatise lies in the way this influence is channeled to manage human resources and particularly how to motivate employees and reward them materially or ethically, as I discussed in chapter II.

From the analysis Gorsky is clearly the CEO that invests more in developing a continuous and dynamic relationship with his employees by encouraging and rewarding them for their uniqueness and in particular for their importance in the company. Second on the list comes McMillon who beyond the incentives and rewards offered on a moral basis, he also uses material incentives and rewards due to the fact that the employees of the company are also stakeholders, and thus he refers to them as partners and stakeholders giving them a completely different purpose and perspective. Third on this list comes Immelt, who makes a series of constant references to the importance of the employees in the company, while fourth comes Schwan with several references to the involvement of employees in the company's success, and fifth comes Stumpf. The rest, though they might make some references, these are not directed to their employees, but this could be justified both by the nature of their speeches and also by the fact that the influence exerted on their employees can often emerge indirectly such as Jobs' speech that inspired thousands of people.

The influence of corporate rhetoric therefore is extremely important, whether it concerns the more immediate material or the more indirect moral and psychological motivation and reward. It can lead to an increase in company profits, thanks to the dedication that motivated employees can bring, whose work is recognized and valued by their superiors. A speech thus, as another tool of HRM, greatly influences employees by seeking to encourage and reward them and is a modern weapon in the arsenal possessed by companies that could really change the rules of the game, a game of 36 ways.

Bibliography

B

Baldoni, J. (2003), *Great communication secrets of great leaders*, McGraw-Hill.

Basu, R. (2009), *Persuasion skills*, BookShaker.

Blyton P. and Turnbull, P. (eds) (1994), *Reassessing Human Resource Management*, London: Sage.

Borg, J. (2007).,*Influence, the art of persuasion*, Kritiki.

Bryman, A. (2004). *Social Research Methods,* Oxford: Oxford University Press.

Buffett, W. (1991), *SALOMON INC – A report by the Chairman on the Company's Position and Outlook,* speech available at: http://www.tilsonfunds.com/BuffettSalomonltr.pdf

C

Castello, I., Lozano, J. (2011), *Searching for new forms of Legitimacy through corporate responsibility rhetoric,* Journal of Business Ethics.

Cialdini, R. (1984), *Influence: The psychology of Persuasion,* Harper Collins.

Cross, G. (1990), *A Bakhtinian exploration of factors affecting the collaborative writing of an executive annual report,* Research in the Teaching of English, 24 (2), 173-203.

D

Darlington, R. (2013), *How to make a good speech,* rogerdarlington.uk.

G

Gates, B. (2013), *Microsoft Research Faculty Summit,* speech available at: http://www.microsoft.com/en-us/news/speeches/2013/07-15billgates.aspx

Gill, C. (1999), *Use of hard and soft models of HRM to illustrate the gap between rhetoric and reality in workforce management,* RMIT Business.

Gorsky, A. (2014), *National Academy Foundation 2014,* speech available at: http://www.jnj.com/our-news-center/Johnson-and-Johnson-CEO-Alex-Gorsky-speaks-to-students-at-the-National-Academy-Foundation-Annual-Benefit

H

Hyland, K. (1998), *Exploring corporate rhetoric: metadiscourse in the CEO's letter,* Journal of Business Communication. 35 (2): 224-245.

I

Immelt, J, (2009) *General Electric's new center will create 1,100 jobs in Detroit,* speech available at: http://online.wsj.com/news/articles/SB124603518881261729

J

Jobs, S. (2005), *Stanford Commencement Speech,* available at: http://news.stanford.edu/news/2005/june15/jobs-061505.html

K

Kartakoullis, N. (2013), *Course Notes MBA 609 Organizations and Human Resources,* Chapters 1-11, University of Nicosia.

Kennedy, George A. (1991), *Aristotle, On Rhetoric: A Theory of Civic*

Discourse, New York: Oxford University Press.

Kohut, G., & Segars, A. (1992), *The president's letter to stockholders: An examination of corporate communication strategy*, The Journal of Business Communication, 29 (1), 7-21.

L

Legge, K. (1995), *Human Resource Management: Rhetorics and Realities*, Basingstoke: Macmillan.

M

Maxwell, J. C. (1998), *Developing the Leader Within You*, Kleidarithmos.

Maxwell, J. C. (2000), *The 21 Indispensable Qualities of a Leader*, Kleidarithmos.

McMillon, D. (2014), *Picking up the Pace of Change for the Customer*, speech available at: http://news.walmart.com/executive-viewpoints/picking-up-the-pace-of-change-for-the-customer

Milgram, S. (1974), *Obedience to Authority; An Experimental View*, Harpercollins.

P

Page, L. (2009), *University of Michigan Commencement Address*, available at: http://googlepress.blogspot.gr/2009/05/larry-pages-university-of-michigan.html

Papalexandri, N. Bourantas and D. (2003), *Human Resource Management*, Editions. Benou.

S

Schwan, S. (2011), *Annual General Meeting*, speech available at: www.roche.com/agm11_sas_e.pdf

Smith, J. (2013), *How to give a great speech,* Forbes.

Stumpf, J. (2014), *Q2 2014 Resuts,* speech available at: http://seekingalpha.com/article/2311495-wells-fargos-wfc-ceo-john-stumpf-on-q2-2014-results-earnings-call-transcript

Suchman, M. (1995), 'Managing legitimacy: Strategic and institutional approaches', Academy of management review.

T

Tillerson, R. (2014), *Meeting the Energy Challenges of the Future: The Role of Industry and Government,* speech available at: http://corporate.exxonmobil.com/en/company/news-and-updates/speeches/meeting-the-energy-challenges-of-the-future

Other Sources

Barisione, M. (2009), "So, What Difference Do Leaders Make? Candidates' Images and the "Conditionality" of Leader Effects on Voting" in Journal of Elections, Public Opinion & Parties, 19: 4, 473-500.

Bucy, Erik P. (2003), "Emotion, Presidential Communication, and Traumatic News: Processing the World Trade Center Attacks" in The Harvard International Journal of Press/Politics 8 (4): 76-96.

Copeland, L., Lamm, W., McKenna, S. J. (1999), *The world's great speeches,* Dover Books.

Crimp, Susan (2011), *The King's speech: A lesson in Perseverance-What King George IV can teach us,* Nook Books ltd.

Dessler, G. (2008), *Human Resource Management,* Prentice Hall.

105

Doob, Leonard W. (1978), *Radio Speeches of World War II*, Ezra Pound ltd.

Dowis, Richard (1999), *The lost art of great speeches: How to write one-How to deliver it,* Ama Publications.

Dutt, Harshvardhan (2010), *Immortal Speeches*, Unicorn books ltd.

Eidenmuller, Michael, E. (2008), *Great speeches for better speaking,* McGrow-Hill Books.

Fairclough, N. (2003), *Analyzing Discourse*, London: Routledge.

Gee, J. P. (1999), *An introduction to discourse analysis: Theory and Method*, Routledge ltd.

Hollenbeck, N. and Wright, G. (2008), *HRM Gaining A Competitive Advantage*, McGraw-Hill.

Jodelet, D. (1989), *Les representations sociales, PUF, Paris.*

Johnson, Whittington and Scholes (2011), Exploring Strategy, 9th Edition, Pearson.

Johnstone, B. (2008), *Discourse Analysis*, Blackwell Publishing.

Kartakoullis, N. (2014), *Course Notes MBA 746 Management of Diversity in Organizations*, Chapters 1-8, the University of Nicosia.

Katula, Richard (2007). "The Art of Political Communication", interview by Victor Tsilonis Intellectum, Interdisciplinary Journal

King, A. (2002), *Leaders' personalities and the outcomes of democratic elections*, Oxford: OUP.

Kinsey, C. (2009), *The nonverbal advantage: Secrets and Science of Body Language,* Goman.

Krippendorff, K. H. (2003), *Content Analysis: An introduction to its Metholodgy,* Sage Publications.

106

Koufidou-Xirotiri, S. (2010), *Management of Human Resources*, Publications Anikoula.

LeBon, G. (1895), *La psychologie des foules*, Paris, Alcan.

MacArthur, B. (2001), *The penguin book of 20th century speeches*, Penguin Books.

Markides, C. C. (1999), *All the right moves: A guide to Crafting Breakthrough Strategy*, Harvard Business School Press.

McGuire, D., Bagher, M., (2010), "Diversity training in organizations: An introduction", Emerald Insight Journal.

Metaxas D. A.I. (2002), *Preliminary remarks on political discourse: Fourteen lessons about style* (3rd Revised edition), Ant. N. Sakoulas.

Michas, D. (2013), *Nationalistic Rhetoric by the Greek far Right: the Metaxas Regime (1936-1940) and the colonels'junta (1967-1974)*, University of Athens.

Milgram, S. (1963), "Behavioral Study of Obedience", in Journal of Abnormal and Social Psychology 67 (4): 371–8.

Milgram, S. (1965), *Some Conditions of Obedience and Disobedience to Authority*, Human Relations 18 (1): 57–76.

Milgram, S. (1974), *The Perils of Obedience*, Harper's Magazine.

Montefiore, Simon Sebag (2008), *Speeches that Changed the World: The Stories and Transcripts of the Moments that Made History*, Quercus Books.

Moscovici, S., Mugny, G., Papastamou, S. (1981) *"Sleeper effect" et / ou effect minoritaire? Etude theorique et experimentale de l'influence sociale a retardement*, Cahiers de psychologie cognitive,1, 199-291.

Navaro, J. , Karlins M. (2008), *What every body is saying*, Harper Collins Books.

107

Neuendorf, Kimberly A. (2002), *The Content analysis guidebook*, Sage Publications.

Norris, P. et al. (1999), *On Message: Communicating the Campaign*, Sage Publications.

Noonan, Peggy (1999), *What I saw at the revolution: On speaking well,* Reagan Books.

O'Connor, R. , Cutler, A. (2008), *Shock Jocks: Hate Speech and Talk Radio: America's ten worst hate talkers and the progressive alternatives*, Alternet books ltd.

Papachristodoulou, C. (2013), "Productivity Up, Wages Down", article in the International investment, finance and professional services magazine in Cyprus.

Papadakis, V.. (2011), *Corporate Strategy*, Publisher Benou.

Papastamou, S. (1989) *Social Influence,* ed. Odysseas, Athens.

Patrick, H., Kumar, V. (2012), "Managing Workplace Diversity: Issues and Challenges", Sage.

Pease, A. Pease, B. (2004), *The definitive book of body language*, Bantam Dell Books.

Perlman, A. M. (1997), *Writing great speeches: Professional Techniques you can use*, Essence of public speaking series.

Ritchie, J. , Lewis, J. (2003), *Qualitative Research Practice: A Guide for Social Science Students*, London: Sage.

Rodway, N., West, S., Bell,E., Marinker, P. (1996), *Great speeches in History*, Naxos books.

Safire, W. (2004), *Lend me your ears: Great speeches in History*, Norton & Company ltd.

Theodoratou, E. (2004), *Management and Organizational Behavior*,

108

Stamoulis.

Weisse, D.S. and Buckley M.R. (1998), "The evolution of the performance appraisal process" in *Journal of Management History,* Vol. 4. No. 3., pp.233-249.

Williams, Hywel (2009), *Great Speeches of our time*, Quercus History.

Annexes

Annex J

Steve Jobs (Apple)

Stanford Commencement Speech, 2005

I am honored to be with you today at your commencement from one of the finest universities in the world. I never graduated from college. Truth be told, this is the closest I've ever gotten to a college graduation. Today I want to tell you three stories from my life. That's it. No big deal. Just three stories.

The first story is about connecting the dots.

I dropped out of Reed College after the first 6 months, but then stayed around as a drop-in for another 18 months or so before I really quit. So why did I drop out?

It started before I was born. My biological mother was a young, unwed college graduate student, and she decided to put me up for adoption. She felt very strongly that I should be adopted by college graduates, so everything was all set for me to be adopted at birth by a lawyer and his wife. Except that when I popped out they decided at the last minute that they really wanted a girl. So my parents, who were on a waiting list, got a call in the middle of the night asking: "We have an unexpected baby boy; do you want him?" They said: "Of course." My biological mother later found out that my mother had never graduated from college and that my father had never graduated from high school. She refused to sign the final adoption papers. She only relented a few months later when my parents promised that I would someday go to college.

And 17 years later I did go to college. But I naively chose a college that was almost as expensive as Stanford, and all of my working-class parents' savings were being spent on my college tuition. After six months, I couldn't see the value in it. I had no idea what I wanted to do with my life and no idea how college was going to help me figure it out. And here I was spending all of the money my parents had saved their entire life. So I decided to drop out and trust that it would all work out OK. It was pretty scary at the time, but looking back it was one of the best decisions I ever made. The minute I dropped out I could stop taking the required classes that didn't interest me, and begin dropping in on the ones that looked interesting.

It wasn't all romantic. I didn't have a dorm room, so I slept on the floor in friends' rooms, I returned coke bottles for the 5¢ deposits to buy food with, and I would walk the 7 miles across town every Sunday night to get one good meal a week at the Hare Krishna temple. I loved it. And much of what I stumbled into by following my curiosity and intuition turned out to be priceless later on. Let me give you one example:

Reed College at that time offered perhaps the best calligraphy instruction in the country. Throughout the campus every poster, every label on every drawer, was beautifully hand calligraphed. Because I had dropped out and didn't have to take the normal classes, I decided to take a calligraphy class to learn how to do this. I learned about serif and san serif typefaces, about varying the amount of space between different letter combinations, about what makes great typography great. It was beautiful, historical, artistically subtle in a way that science can't capture, and I found it fascinating.

None of this had even a hope of any practical application in my life. But ten years later, when we were designing the first Macintosh computer, it all came back to me. And we designed it all into the Mac. It was the first computer with beautiful typography. If I had never dropped in on that single course in college, the Mac would have never had multiple typefaces or proportionally spaced fonts. And since Windows just copied the Mac, it's likely that no personal computer would have them. If I had never dropped out, I would have never dropped in on this calligraphy class, and personal computers might not have the wonderful typography that they do. Of course it was impossible to connect the dots looking forward when I was in college. But it was very, very clear looking backwards ten years later.

Again, you can't connect the dots looking forward; you can only connect them looking backwards. So you have to trust that the dots will somehow connect in your future. You have to trust in something — your gut, destiny, life, karma, whatever. This approach has never let me down, and it has made all the difference in my life.

My second story is about love and loss.

I was lucky — I found what I loved to do early in life. Woz and I started Apple in my parents garage when I was 20. We worked hard, and in 10 years Apple had grown from just the two of us in a garage into a $2 billion company with over 4000 employees. We had just released our finest creation — the Macintosh — a year earlier, and I had just turned 30. And then I got fired. How can you get fired from a company you started? Well, as Apple grew we hired someone who I thought was very talented to run the company with me, and for the first year or so things went well. But then our visions of the future began to diverge and eventually we had a falling out. When we did, our Board of Directors sided with him. So at 30 I was out. And very publicly out. What had been the focus of my entire adult life was gone, and it was devastating.

I really didn't know what to do for a few months. I felt that I had let the previous generation of entrepreneurs down - that I had dropped the baton as it was being passed to me. I met with David Packard and Bob Noyce and tried to apologize for screwing up so badly. I was a very public failure, and I even thought about running away from the valley. But something slowly began to dawn on me — I still loved what I did. The turn of events at Apple had not changed that one bit. I had been rejected, but I was still in love. And so I decided to start over.

I didn't see it then, but it turned out that getting fired from Apple was the best thing that could have ever happened to me. The heaviness of being successful was replaced by the lightness of being a beginner again, less sure about everything. It freed me to enter one of the most creative periods of my life.

During the next five years, I started a company named NeXT, another company named Pixar, and fell in love with an amazing woman who would become my wife. Pixar went on to create the worlds first computer animated feature film, Toy Story, and is now the most successful animation studio in the world. In a remarkable turn of events, Apple bought NeXT, I returned to Apple, and the technology we developed at NeXT is at the heart of Apple's current renaissance. And Laurene and I have a wonderful family together.

I'm pretty sure none of this would have happened if I hadn't been fired from Apple. It was awful tasting medicine, but I guess the patient needed it. Sometimes life hits you in the head with a brick. Don't lose faith. I'm convinced that the only thing that kept me going was that I loved what I did. You've got to find what you love. And that is as true for your work as it is for your lovers. Your work is going to fill a large part of your life, and the only way to be truly satisfied is to do what you believe is great work. And the only way to do great work is to love what you do. If you haven't found it yet, keep looking. Don't settle. As with all matters of the heart, you'll know when you find it. And, like any great relationship, it just gets better and better as the years roll on. So keep looking until you find it. Don't settle.

My third story is about death.

When I was 17, I read a quote that went something like: "If you live each day as if it was your last, someday you'll most certainly be right." It made an impression on me, and since then, for the past 33 years, I have looked in the mirror every morning and asked myself: "If today were the last day of my life, would I want to do what I am about to do today?" And whenever the answer has been "No" for too many days in a row, I know I need to change something.

Remembering that I'll be dead soon is the most important tool I've ever encountered to help me make the big choices in life. Because almost everything — all external expectations, all pride, all fear of embarrassment or failure - these things just fall away in the face of death, leaving only what is truly important. Remembering that you are going to die is the best way I know to avoid the trap of thinking you have something to lose. You are already naked. There is no reason not to follow your heart.

About a year ago I was diagnosed with cancer. I had a scan at 7:30 in the morning, and it clearly showed a tumor on my pancreas. I didn't even know what a pancreas was. The doctors told me this was almost certainly a type of cancer that is incurable, and that I should expect to live no longer than three to six months. My doctor advised me to go home and get my affairs in order, which is doctor's code for prepare to die. It means to try to tell your kids everything you thought you'd have the next 10 years to tell them in just a few months. It means to make sure everything is buttoned up so that it will be as easy as possible for your family. It means to say your goodbyes.

I lived with that diagnosis all day. Later that evening I had a biopsy, where they stuck an endoscope down my throat, through my stomach and into my intestines, put a needle into my pancreas and got a few cells from the tumor. I was sedated, but my wife, who was there, told me that when they viewed the cells under a microscope the doctors started crying because it turned out to be a very rare form of pancreatic cancer that is curable with surgery. I had the surgery and I'm fine now.

This was the closest I've been to facing death, and I hope it's the closest I get for a few more decades. Having lived through it, I can now say this to you with a bit more certainty than when death was a useful but purely intellectual concept:

No one wants to die. Even people who want to go to heaven don't want to die to get there. And yet death is the destination we all share. No one has ever escaped it. And that is as it should be, because Death is very likely the single best invention of Life. It is Life's change agent. It clears out the old to make way for the new. Right now the new is you, but someday not too long from now, you will gradually become the old and be cleared away. Sorry to be so dramatic, but it is quite true.

Your time is limited, so don't waste it living someone else's life. Don't be trapped by dogma — which is living with the results of other people's thinking. Don't let the noise of others' opinions drown out your own inner voice. And most important, have the courage to follow your heart and intuition. They somehow already know what you truly want to become. Everything else is secondary.

When I was young, there was an amazing publication called The Whole Earth Catalog, which was one of the bibles of my generation. It was created by a fellow named Stewart Brand not far from here in Menlo Park, and he brought it to life with his poetic touch. This was in the late 1960's, before personal computers and desktop publishing, so it was all made with typewriters, scissors, and polaroid cameras. It was sort of like Google in paperback form, 35 years before Google came along: it was idealistic, and overflowing with neat tools and great notions.

Stewart and his team put out several issues of The Whole Earth Catalog, and then when it had run its course, they put out a final issue. It was the mid-1970s, and I was your age. On the back cover of their final issue was a photograph of an early morning country road, the kind you might find yourself hitchhiking on if you were so adventurous. Beneath it were the words: "Stay Hungry. Stay Foolish." It was their farewell message as they signed off. Stay Hungry. Stay Foolish. And I have always wished that for myself. And now, as you graduate to begin a new, I wish that for you.

Stay Hungry. Stay Foolish.

Thank you all very much.

Annex JJ

Rex Tillerson (Exxon Mobil)

Meeting the Energy Challenges of the Future: The Role of Industry and Government

Rex Tillerson

Chairman and Chief Executive Officer

21st World Petroleum Congress

Moscow, Russian Federation

"Your Excellencies ... distinguished guests ... honored friends ... and valued colleagues.

It is a pleasure to once again address the World Petroleum Congress.

The World Petroleum Congress has established itself as one of our industry's premier gatherings.

The WPC provides us with the opportunity to look to the future and discuss how government, industry, and society can work together to deliver the energy the world needs to grow and advance. And as the theme of this Congress suggests, we seek not just to deliver the energy the world needs, but to do so in a way that is safe and environmentally responsible.

It is especially fitting that the 21st meeting of the World Petroleum

Congress is being convened in Russia – the No. 1 crude oil producer in the world, and a leading supplier of natural gas.

On behalf of delegates from all over the world, I want to thank our Russian hosts and the people of Moscow for their warm welcome.

The purpose of this panel is to discuss "energy strategies for a growing world." Building these sound energy strategies begins with understanding the sources and magnitude of the challenges we must meet.

First and foremost, we must recognize that the global need for energy is projected to grow – and grow significantly.

ExxonMobil projects that increases in population, along with growing trade and development, will increase global energy demand by about 30 percent between now and the year 2040. To put this number in perspective: It will be like adding more than the combined current energy demand of Russia and India, all of Africa, Latin America, and the Middle East.

We must also recognize that the vast majority of this growth in population and energy demand will take place in developing economies.

These fundamental facts mean that every discussion of energy and energy policy has a humanitarian dimension.

According to the latest figures on global energy poverty, about one in five human beings still has no access to electricity. And two out of five people must rely on biomass such as wood, charcoal, or animal waste for their basic cooking and heating needs, which has far-reaching consequences for their health and quality of life.

The key to lifting people out of this poverty – and to increasing hope and opportunity for billions, including those yet to be born – is to expand the supplies and availability of modern sources of energy.

Simply put, the global need for energy we see today – and the growth in demand we anticipate in the decades ahead – will require the world to pursue all sources of energy, wherever and whenever they are economically competitive.

In addition, there is a second element to every discussion of energy and energy policy: We must pursue strategies that reflect wise environmental stewardship.

This means we must invest, innovate, and relentlessly advance the technologies and techniques that promote energy efficiency, improve environmental performance, and reduce the greenhouse gas and air pollution emissions associated with increased energy use.

The good news is that our industry has proven, throughout our history, that we can expand supplies in safe, secure, and environmentally responsible ways.

Because of our investments, innovations, and cooperation, we can point to extraordinary successes.

Over the last three decades alone, we have taken on deepwater and ultra-deepwater challenges, we have developed new techniques to unlock unconventional oil and natural gas, and we continue to expand on our historic achievements in the Arctic and sub-Arctic to provide the energy the world needs.

These new sources of energy – and our technological advances and performance – have, in turn, powered the global economy, helped nations progress, and improved the individual lives and futures of hundreds of millions of people. And as the world has advanced, every sector has become more energy efficient. At ExxonMobil, we believe that this trend will hold in the decades ahead, making the No. 1 "source" for new energy, energy efficiency itself.

This morning, I will briefly discuss each of these successes – and the policy lessons we can learn from them for taking on the energy challenges of the future.

One of our industry's most extraordinary advances has been in the deepwater. Advanced technologies have enabled unprecedented offshore exploration and production. A generation ago, my generation of engineers worked at drafting tables with hand drawings of design specs for drilling rigs, while geoscientists were hand-interpreting seismic shoots.

Today, of course, we use high-speed, sophisticated computers to find resources and design rigs that can operate in water depths of more than 10,000 feet, drilling wells that extend five miles below the ocean floor.

With each passing year, our industry continues to advance the technologies and processes we employ – enabling us to go deeper, more quickly, more accurately, and more safely than ever before.

As a result, we project that in the period from 2010 to 2040, deepwater oil production worldwide will grow 150 percent. And deepwater contributions to global liquids supply will rise from 6 to 12 percent.

Our offshore capabilities now represent some of the greatest engineering marvels in human history. But these technological achievements do not stand alone. They have been accompanied by striking advancements in other parts of our industry.

In less than a decade, the modern energy map has been rewritten by technological breakthroughs in North America.

Our industry's integration of hydraulic fracturing and horizontal drilling has made it possible to develop North America's shale gas and tight oil – bountiful resources found in dense rock formations.

Consider that between 2005 and 2014 alone, U.S. production of crude oil and natural gas has risen by close to 70 percent and 45 percent, respectively, which reflects growing tight oil and shale gas production.

With this newfound abundance, North America is reminding the world of the fundamental importance of energy and the extraordinary contributions our industry can make in individual nations – and individual lives.

Thanks to vast new supplies of unconventional natural gas, for instance, we are helping deliver economic growth as well as environmental benefits in the United States.

New sources of oil and natural gas are driving U.S. economic growth, supporting millions of jobs, and spurring significant gains – and expansions – in manufacturing.

In addition to these economic benefits, abundant and reliable natural gas has helped reduce U.S. carbon-dioxide emissions to levels not seen since the 1990s. Even more remarkably – it has been achieved in an economy that is 50 percent larger than in the 1990s with 50 million more energy consumers.

This progress reflects the substantial benefits of a free-market approach to energy development and use.

As many in this room already know, our industry is still in the exploratory stages of applying our recent breakthrough technologies and risk-management techniques to regions outside North America.

Government and industry continue to assess the size of the global endowment of unconventional natural gas. At ExxonMobil we are optimistic about areas for potential development in Asia, Latin America, Northern Africa, parts of Europe – and here in Russia, in Western Siberia.

For the world, new supplies of oil and natural gas in North America will provide diversity and flexibility to the global energy portfolio – and demonstrate that our industry has taken a leadership position in environmental stewardship.

As our industry works to meet the energy challenges of the future, there is another area of promise and potential: the Arctic.

The Arctic is one of the world's largest remaining regions of undiscovered conventional oil and natural gas resources.

And, contrary to some claims, it is not unfamiliar territory for our

120

industry. The Arctic has been a major oil and natural gas producer for decades.

Ninety years ago, our company first entered the Arctic. Since then, our industry has proven, time and time again, that we can develop these resources safely and responsibly, managing the region's unique challenges.

For example, ExxonMobil has partnered with Rosneft and other international co-venturers, to produce oil and natural gas offshore Sakhalin Island for more than a decade. The Sakhalin-1 fields continue to produce at a current rate of approximately 7.3 million metric tons of oil and approximately 2.4 billion standard cubic meters of gas a year. To date, more than 61 million tons of oil has been produced and 13 billion cubic meters of natural gas have been delivered since the start of operations in 2005.

We have produced these new supplies of energy in harsh, arctic conditions, setting horizontal-drilling records while upholding a world-class safety and environmental record.

In the years ahead, we look forward to taking advances achieved in these cutting-edge successes in Far East Russia and building upon them to unlock new supplies of oil and natural gas in the Kara Sea and beyond.

Our industry has the ability to build on these achievements by continuing to pioneer new technologies, deploy best practices, and ensure safer operations across the entire energy supply and value chain. And by applying extensive scientific research and making operational accommodations, our industry has shown we can expand supplies of energy from the Arctic and sub-Arctic as well as protect wildlife and biodiversity.

All three of these industry achievements – deepwater, unconventionals, and the Arctic – provide lessons on how to construct and maintain "energy strategies for a growing world." The strategies of the future must reward long-term planning, sustained investment, and constant

121

innovation.

No matter where our industry goes in the world, we will need new technologies to expand supplies and enhance environmental performance and protection.

Whether we seek to expand global supplies of energy in North America, South America, Africa, Asia, Europe, or Australia, the most effective path to investment and innovation is for government and industry to understand their specific roles and responsibilities.

Our industry respects the role of government. We recognize that government is uniquely suited to promote the rule of law, provide a clear regulatory pathway, and hold companies accountable. In addition, government is critical to establishing the level playing field that enables companies to compete – and consumers to win.

In short, government leaders are responsible for putting in place the sound and stable regulatory and tax policies that enable investment, cooperation, and risk management to flourish. And only that foundation can ensure there is incentive for industry to invest in the research, development, and deployment of evolutionary and revolutionary technologies.

To meet the energy challenges of the future, our industry must maintain its positive role in public dialogue.

We must communicate with the public and policymakers about how we can achieve our shared aspirations to expand opportunity for all peoples and to promote environmental stewardship in every nation.

We must also communicate the consequences that follow when governments fail to establish or maintain sound policies. We know from experience that heavy-handed market interventions by government, burdensome regulations, or taxpayer subsidies that favor companies or industries can undermine the technological advancements that enable us to meet the world's energy needs safely, efficiently, and responsibly.

The U.S. unconventional revolution has shown that we can expand supplies and reduce air pollution and carbon emissions. With sound policies, our industry can apply new technologies and techniques to unlock cleaner-burning natural gas all around the world. As we do so, we can meet growing energy needs, while reducing emissions levels. And with sound policies industry can continue to develop technologies to produce and use oil more efficiently – especially in the transportation sector where growing energy needs are so critical to trade, work, and advancement.

It is clear the world will need to pursue all economic sources of energy – including deepwater, shale gas and tight oil, and conventional sources in the Arctic. And by relentlessly improving our technologies, we can improve our environmental performance at every link in the energy chain, increase energy efficiency in every economic sector, and promote environmental care and progress in every nation.

The oil and natural gas industry will continue to play an essential – and pivotal – role in shaping the world's future. And indeed, even at a time when challenges have befallen some important producing areas, the industry at large – both non-OPEC and OPEC players – has contributed in the reliable supplies to consumers the world over.

With government and industry fulfilling our respective roles and responsibilities, we can help alleviate poverty, raise living standards, and create economic opportunity for billions of people. And by continuing our industry's dialogue with the public and policymakers, we can put in place energy policies that enable investments and technological advancements on every frontier and in every sector. Such long-term strategies will help government, industry, and society each play its part in building a brighter future for all in a growing world.

I thank you for your kind attention."

Annex JJJ

Larry Page (Google)

University of Michigan Commencement Address 2009

Class of 2009! First I'd like you to get up, wave and cheer your supportive family and friends! Show your love!

It is a great honor for me to be here today.

Now wait a second. I know: that's such a cliché. You're thinking: every graduation speaker says that – It's a great honor. But, in my case, it really is so deeply true – being here is more special and more personal for me than most of you know. I'd like to tell you why.

A long time ago, in the cold September of 1962, there was a Steven's co-op at this very university. That co-op had a kitchen with a ceiling that had been cleaned by student volunteers every decade or so. Picture a college girl named Gloria, climbing up high on a ladder, struggling to clean that filthy ceiling. Standing on the floor, a young boarder named Carl was admiring the view. And that's how they met. They were my parents, so I suppose you could say I'm a direct result of that kitchen chemistry experiment, right here at Michigan. My Mom is here with us today, and we should probably go find the spot and put a plaque up on the ceiling that says: "Thanks Mom and Dad!"

Everyone in my family went to school here at Michigan: me, my brother, my Mom and Dad – all of us. My Dad actually got the quantity discount: all three and a half of his degrees are from here. His Ph.D. was in Communication Science because they thought Computers were just a passing fad. He earned it 44 years ago. He and Mom made a big sacrifice for that. They argued at times over pennies, while raising my newborn brother. Mom typed my Dad's dissertation by hand. This velvet hood I'm wearing, this was my Dad's. And this diploma, just like the one you're are about to get, that was my Dad's. And my underwear, that was... oh never mind.

My father's father worked in the Chevy plant in Flint, Michigan. He was an assembly line worker. He drove his two children here to Ann Arbor, and told them: That is where you're going to go to college. Both his kids did graduate from Michigan. That was the American dream. His daughter, Beverly, is with us today. My Grandpa used to carry an "Alley Oop" hammer – a heavy iron pipe with a hunk of lead melted on the end. The workers made them during the sit-down strikes to protect themselves. When I was growing up, we used that hammer whenever we needed to pound a stake or something into the ground. It is wonderful that most people don't need to carry a heavy blunt object for protection anymore. But just in case, I have it here.

My Dad became a professor at uh... Michigan State, and I was an incredibly lucky boy. A professor's life is pretty flexible, and he was able to spend oodles of time raising me. Could there be a better upbringing than university brat?

What I'm trying to tell you is that this is WAY more than just a homecoming for me. It's not easy for me to express how proud I am to be here, with my Mom, my brother and my wife Lucy, and with all of you, at this amazing institution that is responsible for my very existence. I am thrilled for all of you, and I'm thrilled for your families and friends, as all of us join the great, big Michigan family I feel I've been a part of all of my life.

What I'm also trying to tell you is that I know exactly what it feels like to be sitting in your seat, listening to some old gasbag give a long-winded commencement speech. Don't worry. I'll be brief.

I have a story about following dreams. Or maybe more accurately, it's a story about finding a path to make those dreams real.

You know what it's like to wake up in the middle of the night with a vivid dream? And you know how, if you don't have a pencil and pad by the bed to write it down, it will be completely gone the next morning?

Well, I had one of those dreams when I was 23. When I suddenly woke up, I was thinking: what if we could download the whole web, and just keep the links and... I grabbed a pen and started writing! Sometimes it is important to wake up and stop dreaming. I spent the middle of that night scribbling out the details and convincing myself it would work. Soon after, I told my advisor, Terry Winograd, it would take a couple of weeks to download the web – he nodded knowingly, fully aware it would take much longer but wise enough to not tell me. The optimism of youth is often underrated! Amazingly, I had no thought of building a search engine. The idea wasn't even on the radar. But, much later we happened upon a better way of ranking webpages to make a really great search engine, and Google was born. When a really great dream shows up, grab it!

When I was here at Michigan, I had actually been taught how to make dreams real! I know it sounds funny, but that is what I learned in a summer camp converted into a training program called Leadershape. Their slogan is to have a "healthy disregard for the impossible". That program encouraged me to pursue a crazy idea at the time: I wanted to build a personal rapid transit system on campus to replace the buses. It was a futuristic way of solving our transportation problem. I still think a lot about transportation – you never loose a dream, it just incubates as a hobby. Many things that people labor hard to do now, like cooking, cleaning, and driving will require much less human time in the future. That is, if we "have a healthy disregard for the impossible" and actually build new solutions.

I think it is often easier to make progress on mega-ambitious dreams. I know that sounds completely nuts. But, since no one else is crazy enough to do it, you have little competition. There are so few people this crazy that I feel like I know them all by first name. They all travel as if they are pack dogs and stick to each other like glue. The best people want to work the big challenges. That is what happened with Google. Our mission is to organize the world's information and make it universally accessible and useful. How can that not get you excited? But we almost didn't start Google because my co-founder Sergey and I were too worried about dropping out of our Ph.D. program. You are probably on the right track if you feel like a sidewalk worm during a rainstorm! That is about how we felt after we maxed out three credit cards buying hard disks off the back of a truck. That was the first hardware for Google. Parents and friends: more credit cards always help. What is the one sentence summary of how you change the world? Always work hard on something uncomfortably exciting!

As a Ph.D. student, I actually had three projects I wanted to work on. Thank goodness my advisor said, "why don't you work on the web for a while". He gave me some seriously good advice because the web was really growing with people and activity, even in 1995! Technology and especially the internet can really help you be lazy. Lazy? What I mean is a group of three people can write software that millions can use and enjoy. Can three people answer the phone a million times a day? Find the leverage in the world, so you can be more lazy!

Overall, I know it seems like the world is crumbling out there, but it is actually a great time in your life to get a little crazy, follow your curiosity, and be ambitious about it. Don't give up on your dreams. The world needs you all!

So here's my final story:

On a day like today, you might feel exhilarated — like you've just been shot out of a cannon at the circus – and even invincible. Don't ever forget that incredible feeling. But also: always remember that the moments we have with friends and family, the chances we have to do things that might make a big difference in the world, or even to make a small difference to someone you love — all those wonderful chances

127

that life gives us, life also takes away. It can happen fast, and a whole lot sooner than you think.

In late March 1996, soon after I had moved to Stanford for grad school, my Dad had difficultly breathing and drove to the hospital. Two months later, he died. And that was it. I was completely devastated. Many years later, after a startup, after falling in love, and after so many of life's adventures, I found myself thinking about my Dad. Lucy and I were far away in a steaming hot village walking through narrow streets. There were wonderful friendly people everywhere, but it was a desperately poor place – people used the bathroom inside and it flowed out into the open gutter and straight into the river. We touched a boy with a limp leg, the result of paralysis from polio. Lucy and I were in rural India – one of the few places where Polio still exists. Polio is transmitted fecal to oral, usually through filthy water. Well, my Dad had Polio. He went on a trip to Tennessee in the first grade and caught it. He was hospitalized for two months and had to be transported by military DC-3 back home – his first flight. My Dad wrote, "Then, I had to stay in bed for over a year, before I started back to school". That is actually a quote from his fifth grade autobiography. My Dad had difficulty breathing his whole life, and the complications of Polio are what took him from us too soon. He would have been very upset that Polio still persists even though we have a vaccine. He would have been equally upset that back in India we had polio virus on our shoes from walking through the contaminated gutters that spread the disease. We were spreading the virus with every footstep, right under beautiful kids playing everywhere. The world is on the verge of eliminating polio, with 328 people infected so far this year. Let's get it done soon. Perhaps one of you will do that.

My Dad was valedictorian of Flint Mandeville High School 1956 class of about 90 kids. I happened across his graduating speech recently, and it blew me away. 53 years ago at his graduation my Dad said: "…we are entering a changing world, one of automation and employment change where education is an economic necessity. We will have increased periods of time to do as we wish, as our work week and retirement age continue to decline. … We shall take part in, or witness, developments in science, medicine, and industry that we cannot dream of today. … It

128

is said that the future of any nation can be determined by the care and preparation given to its youth. If all the youths of America were as fortunate in securing an education as we have been, then the future of the United States would be even more bright than it is today."

If my Dad was alive today, the thing I think he would be most happy about is that Lucy and I have a baby in the hopper. I think he would have been annoyed that I hadn't gotten my Ph.D. yet (thanks, Michigan!). Dad was so full of insights, of excitement about new things, that to this day, I often wonder what he would think about some new development. If he were here today – well, it would be one of the best days of his life. He'd be like a kid in a candy store. For a day, he'd be young again.

Many of us are fortunate enough to be here with family. Some of us have dear friends and family to go home to. And who knows, perhaps some of you, like Lucy and I, are dreaming about future families of your own. Just like me, your families brought you here, and you brought them here. Please keep them close and remember: they are what really matters in life.

Thanks, Mom; Thanks, Lucy.

And thank you, all, very much.

Annex IV

Bill Gates (Microsoft)

2013 Microsoft Research Faculty Summit.

Well, good morning. It's great to be here. I haven't been here for over five years so it's great to see the way this event has grown. And I think it's fair to say that we're in a golden age of computer science. The original vision of Microsoft that we had a dream about what software could do if we had infinite computing and infinite storage; that almost is our reality today. And so it's amazing for me to see how that's being applied, whether it's user interface, with vision, speech, pen, with modeling in rich data areas with machine learning. And it really seems like that idea, the powerful assistant that can help us get things done, help us drive deep insights, that the progress we'll make in the next 5 years and 10 years will be really unbelievable. Even our friends in the hardware industry are giving us better screens, better sensors, things that let us exercise the magic of software. And for Microsoft, that means taking something like Office and going from documents to deep insights, taking something like search and going from links to answers to task solutions. So software, you know, has only achieved a very small portion of what we want it to do and even you could say what we need it to do. If you look at things like climate modeling, energy innovation, so much that this field has to contribute to solving broad science problems. I thought just as a kickoff, I'd give you four examples of things that I work on at the foundation before we go on to the Q&A, and really highlight how in each of those areas it's software and digital approaches that are letting us be very ambitious.

130

The Gates Foundation really focuses in two areas. One is education, that's primarily focused in the United States. And then the other is a series of global issues focused on the poorest in the world, including disease. That's by far the biggest thing, over 2 billion a year that we spend there; agriculture, finance, sanitation, a variety of things that relate to the poorest.

And so let's just start with education. Last week, I was down with Sal Khan talking about the work he is doing with his Khan Academy website. The foundation has been the biggest funder of various MOOCs [massive open online courses] to see what can be done, not just for the type of people, the more elite students who are probably the first-time users of those systems, but also looking down at the students who may not make it through college, where remedial math, remedial writing classes really discourage them and they have a hard time thinking through what are their skill sets and how do they match up to a profession that might be high paying. They have a hard time organizing their time and their finances to make sure that they're getting through, for those things to work. And what we're seeing is that not only at the course level itself to help model what the student knows and interact with them in a way that is encouraging, but even in that idea of the career decision; what are the credentials they need, or even monitoring to see if they don't show up for a class, immediately engaging with them ideally in an inexpensive digital way but perhaps knowing that the counselor needs to go in there and talk to them about their career goals. The United States has the highest dropout rate in higher education of any rich country. We actually are fairly middle of the road in terms of the percentage that go to higher ed, but we drop to below average in the percentage that graduate because of our uniquely high dropout rates. And of course at the same time, we have a financial conundrum that if we're going to give more people college education, the cost is going up and the financial resources for that aren't generally available. So taking the courses, things like math, letting you know where you are, making it more personalized, drawing in your teacher to see what you've been doing, a lot of excitement there, and so, you know, we're funding that.

Over in the health area, we work on diseases like HIV, malaria, all the

131

childhood killers, pneumonia, diarrhea and for us disease modeling is a big area. We have a gigantic Windows cluster machine where we do stochastic modeling. We built a group of about 25 people that work with other universities on disease modeling, so things like weather, transport, mosquito populations, immune system state -- a very rich model because our goal with a couple diseases, first with polio and then with malaria, is to actually go for total eradication. Now, so understanding what tools do we need, drugs, bed nets, killing mosquitoes in the case of malaria. In the case of polio, it's looking at the genetics of the virus, seeing where it's spreading, understand how the kids move around, what we need to do to boost their immune systems. Those tools will make all the difference in terms of developing the confidence in what we do and coming up with the right tactics out in the field.

Another example is agriculture. There it's genetics, where we're looking at the crops, coming up with some very important improvements. We're putting things like vitamin A and iron into the crops. Bananas in Uganda within about three years we'll have those micronutrients, that's very important. We're putting in disease resistance. A big crop in Africa is cassava. There're two diseases that are now wiping out about 30 percent of the production. And it's not just a numeric thing that, you know, 30 percent across the continent; it's some farmers who this crop which is sort of their backup crop they have a complete wipe out, and that means that they really are destitute -- not able to feed their family. Well, by putting in some additional genes, in this case an RNAi interference technique, we're able to block these diseases.

And so, how do you get that out, how do you make sure people feel from a regulatory point of view that's going to be safe and available -- a very tough challenge. And we also in crops put in more drought resistance. We put in -- in rice, a thing called submergence tolerance. That's actually one of our great success stories. We now have 18 million farmers in Asia who plant a variety of rice that if it gets submerged will just stop -- not die off, and then when the water goes down it resumes growing. All the rice varieties before that, when they were submerged they would just die off. That's a good one because people can see how magical it is and so it's had a higher rate of adaption than any of the new crop work that we've done.

And finally, an area to mention is in finance. Of course, consumers in the rich world have account balances and credit cards and things that let them plan ahead, and borrow money when they need to. For the very poorest, those institutions don't exist. And now there's been an attempt to microfinance to create some of that, at least on the loan side. It hasn't been good on the saving side. It hasn't been able to embody programs that are unique for things like agriculture and retail. And as we move to cellphone-based digital currency though, the transition cost can be brought down a lot. One of the problems with microfinance is that the interest rates, even if you don't have defaults, because of the processing overhead is well over 15 percent a year. And so, it's very difficult to find economic activity that can overcome that cost structure. When we move it into digital form, then we get it down to below 5 percent. And so it makes a big difference. But also it allows us to be creative, so that when I sell my crop after the harvest, it advises me to set aside the money for the seed and the fertilizer, and even makes that deposit. So, it gives me some way to look forward to what I need to do, to make sure I'm managing my money in the right way.

We have one country, which is Kenya, that the economy is moving to digital currency. It's called M-PESA, something that the foundation and the U.K. Aid Department were behind. And it's amazing; once it gets to critical mass. It's like, you know, credit cards or debit cards but it's -- you can transfer person-to-person, a small shopkeeper can set up, and we can instrument what's going on with that economy in a way that was impossible in a currency-based approach, and lots of innovative products are coming out that serve the very poorest.

So even progress for the 2 billion most in need in health and agriculture and all these different areas really are going to be dependent on the kind of rich, computer science software-driven advances that you work on. So that I think the opportunities are quite phenomenal, particularly as we can get commercial companies like Microsoft working with you and take your great work and get it out into products that can help millions of people.

133

Annex V

Warren Buffett (Berkshire Hathaway)

SALOMON INC – A report by the Chairman on the Company's Position and Outlook

To the Shareholders of Salomon Inc:

In this report, I want not only to tell you about Salomon Inc's third-quarter results but also to give you my thinking as to where the company must head.

From announcements we have made and from the media you have learned about the events that led to my appointment as interim Chairman of Salomon Inc on August 18. We have since continued to investigate Salomon's past actions in the Government securities market and in other areas as well. Our conclusion so far: A few Salomon employees behaved egregiously-a fact that will prove costly to you as shareholders-but the misconduct and misjudgments were limited to those few. In short, I believe that we had an extremely serious problem, but not a pervasive one.

Since August 18, we have installed rules and procedures at Salomon Brothers Inc, our securities subsidiary, that we think set a standard for the industry. In addition, we have begun to monitor what goes on in Salomon Brothers in new ways-for example, by setting up a Compliance Committee of the Board-and expect in that area also to be a leader. Even so, an atmosphere encouraging exemplary behavior is probably even more important than rules, necessary though these are. During my tenure as Chairman, I will consider myself the firm's chief compliance officer and I have asked all 9,000 of Salomon's employees to assist me in that effort. I have also urged them to be guided by a test that goes beyond rules: Contemplating any business act, an employee should ask himself whether he would be willing to see it immediately described by an informed and critical reporter on the front page of his local paper, there to be read by his spouse, children and friends. At Salomon we simply want no part of any activities that pass legal tests but that we, as citizens, would find offensive.

Ordinary operations during the third quarter produced excellent profits, in large part because of exceptionally favorable trends in the fixed-income markets. I need to alert you, however, to two major adjustments that affected the bottom line, one negatively, one positively.

In the first instance, we have set up a pre-tax legal reserve of $200 million for potential settlements, judgments, penalties, fines, litigation expense and other related costs. In the second instance, the compensation expense we have recorded for Salomon Brothers is about $110 million less than what might normally be expected. Because certain legal costs may not be deductible for tax purposes, different tax rates apply to the two unusual items. Their combined effect, therefore, was a reduction in net income of about $75 million.

I would like to elaborate on each of these unusual items, beginning with legal costs. No one can now estimate with any degree of certainty what the eventual direct costs of Salomon's past misdeeds and misjudgments will be to the company. (There are also very important secondary costs, such as loss of business and increased funding, costs; but, as I shall detail later, there may additionally be' secondary benefits, perhaps substantial.). Whatever these costs are , however, our large equity base - $ 4 billion – virtually insures that they will not be crippling.

We will pay any fines or penalties with dispatch and we will also try to settle valid legal claims promptly. However, we will litigate invalid or inflated claims, of which there will be many, to whatever extent necessary. That is, we will make appropriate amends for past conduct but we will be no one's patsy.

Accounting rules require that we review the size of our reserve with Our auditors and counsel. That has been, done and-based on the limited amount of information presently available-they agree with the present estimate. We will make upward or downward adjustments to the reserve ~s information and events clarify the situation.

Most of you have read articles about the high levels of compensation at Salomon Brothers. Some of you have also read discussions of incentive compensation that I have written in the Berkshire Hathaway annual report. In those, I have said that I believe a rational incentive compensation plan to be an excellent way to reward managers, and I have also embraced the concept of truly extraordinary pay for extraordinary managerial performance. I continue to subscribe to those views. But the problem at Salomon Brothers has been a compensation plan that was irrational in certain crucial respects.

One irrationality has been compensation levels that overall have been too high in relation to overall results. For example, last year the securities unit earned about 10% oil equity capital-far tinder the average earned by American business-yet 106 individuals who worked for the unit earned $1 million or more. Many of these people pet-formed exceedingly well and clearly deserved their pay. But the overall result made no sense: Though 1990 operating profits. before compensation were flat versus 1989, pay jumped by more than $120 million. And that, of course, meant earnings for shareholders fell by the same amount. A related irrationality is connected to the lopsided way in which Salomon has earned its profits-a matter, indeed, on which Salomon's directors were not supplied sufficient information. The data I now have available show that Salomon's lackluster overall profits of recent years resulted from a combination of excellent earnings in a few areas of the business-operating in an honest and ethical manner, it should be added-with inadequate or non-existent earnings at the remainder. Yet the compensation plan did not take this extreme unevenness into account. In

136

effect, the fine performance of some People Subsidized truly out-sized rewards for others. It would be understandable if a private partnership opted For such all egalitarian, share-the-wealth system. But Salomon is a publicly owned company depending on vast amounts of shareholders' capital. In such an operation, it is appropriate that the excess earnings of the exceptional performers-that is, what they generate beyond what they are justly paid-go to the stockholders.

Of course, it is difficult to quantify performance in many vital jobs, such as compliance, audit, funding, and research. For these activities, and for operational and support jobs as well, Salomon employees should normally be paid in line with industry standards, whether profits are high or low. Our compensation plans must also both reward cooperative, for-the-good-of-the-firm behavior and recognize that some business units earn relatively little in profits but deliver valuable, if hard to quantify, collateral benefits to the firm.

All that said, there remain many jobs for which performance can be concretely measured and ought to, be. In these, employees who produce exceptional results for the firm, while operating both honorably and without excessive risk, should expect to receive first-class compensation. On the other hand, employees producing mediocre returns for owners should expect their pay to reflect this shortfall. In the past that has neither been the expectation at Salomon nor the practice.

Salomon Inc's directors have decided that total compensation at Salomon Brothers in 1991 will be slightly below the level of 1990. Through June 30, 1991, however, compensation accruals had been made at a rate that considerably exceeded 1990's. Therefore, a $110 million downward adjustment of the accrual was made in the third quarter.

In 1991 and in the future, the top-paid people at Salomon Brothers will get much of their compensation in the form of stock, pursuant to the Equity Partnership Plat] (EPP), which previous management instituted last year and which we heartily applaud. The EPP motivates managers to think like owners, since it obliges them to hold the stock they buy for at least five years and therefore exposes them to the risks of the business as well as the opportunities. Contrast this arrangement with stock-option plans, in which managers commit money only if the game has already been won and then often move quickly to sell their shares.

In Salomon Brothers' business, which combines leverage with earnings volatility, it is particularly necessary and appropriate that the financial equation applying personally to managers be comparable to that applying to the ordinary shareholder. We wish to see the unit's managers become wealthy through ownership, not by simply free-riding on the ownership of others, I think in fact that ownership can in time bring our best managers substantial wealth, perhaps in amounts well beyond what they now think possible.

To avoid dilution, the trustee of the EPP purchases stock for the plan in the market and at some point in the future the company may itself elect to make stock repurchases to reduce the shares outstanding. Within a relatively few years Salomon Inc's key employees could own 25% or more of the business, purchased with their own compensation. The better job each employee does for the company, the more stock he or she will own.

Our pay-for-performance philosophy will undoubtedly cause some managers to leave. But very importantly, this same philosophy may induce the top performers to stay, since these people may identify themselves as .350 hitters about to be paid appropriately instead of seeing their just rewards partially assigned to lesser performers. Indeed, I am pleased to report that certain of our very best managers have already asked that the EPP be modified to allow them to substantially increase the proportion of their earnings that can be invested through the plan.

Were an abnormal number of people to leave the firm, the results would not necessarily be bad. Other men and women who share our thinking and values would then be given added responsibilities and opportunities. In the end we must have people to match our principles, not the reverse.

Our September 30th balance sheet totals are down by over $37 billion from those of June 30th-from $134 billion to $97 billion. The pace of

138

change, however, has been even more dramatic than these figures indicate: Total assets on August 16, just before I became Chairman, were about $150 billion.

In Salomon Brothers' business, I should point out, substantial amounts of borrowed money are necessary and proper. We will continue, for example, to make large, short- term commitments to finance underwritings and block-purchases of equities, mortgages and bonds. Indeed, we expect to be a leader in these fields.

Nonetheless, we have deliberately brought our balance sheet totals down to reduce our leverage, and you will see the totals come down further in the months ahead. I am no fan of huge leverage in general, and in Salomon's case I believe that the swelling of the balance sheet that took place in the past was often done for the sake of all-too-marginal returns. Larger totals can actually lead to smaller profits: Undisciplined decision-making is a frequent consequence of ultra-easy access to funding, as both commercial and investment banks have learned in recent years.

One final, reassuring point about the balance sheet: Salomon's previous management strongly favored conservative reserving. Significant allowances for various risks of the business have been-and will be-maintained.

Phibro, the other major business owned by Salomon Inc, is achieving only mediocre profits this year after a terrific performance in 1990. Many investors recognize Phibro as a world leader in the trading of oil and related derivative instruments but are unaware of the magnitude of Phibro's oil refinery business. Phibro's four refineries typically process about 330,000 barrels of oil per day, which is equal to more than a third of the U.S. refining output of Exxon. But refining spreads this year have been narrow and Phibro's profits from this business have fallen sharply.

The company has made excellent progress, however, with White Nights (WNJE), its Siberian oil project, in which our Russian partner is Varyeganneftegaz Production Association. I have met with Anatoli Sivak, the talented Director General of Varyeganneftegaz and Chairman of WNJE, and share his enthusiasm about developments to date.

Essentially, this venture is drilling new wells and reworking existing wells in three designated fields. In payment, it is entitled to the incremental output it succeeds in producing over what the output would have been had WNJE's development not occurred.

To date, WNJE has undertaken 37 workovers, of which 25 were successful. Additionally, one new well has recently been completed. In aggregate, these wells have increased production by about 4,700 barrels per day. WNJE is receiving hard currency for its oil and the pace of drilling will accelerate. Though the project entails political and petroleum engineering risks, WNJE's potential is large.

In recent years both Salomon Inc, the parent, and Phibro Energy have been treated by top management as adjuncts to Salomon Brothers. That was understandable, given that the managers of the parent came from the securities unit. Now, however, we are viewing Salomon Inc as the owner of two independent and substantial businesses, each of which will be measured by return on the equity capital it requires.

I noted earlier that there may well be future benefits that arise from our current problems. We have the prospect of correcting certain weaknesses at Salomon Brothers that were likely to remain unaddressed absent a change in management; meanwhile, the firm's strengths in large part remain intact. Though earnings volatility will always be high, Salomon Inc has the capacity amid favorable market conditions to earn substantial slims. Furthermore, I believe that we can earn these Superior returns playing aggressively in the center of the court, without resorting to close-to-the-line acrobatics. Good profits simply are not inconsistent with good behavior.

Our goal is going to be that stated many decades ago by J.P. Morgan, who wished to see his bank transact "first-class business-in a first-class way." We will judge ourselves in fact not only by the business we do, but also by the business we decline to do. As is the case at all large organizations, there will be mistakes at Salomon and even failures, but to the best of our ability we will acknowledge our errors quickly and

140

correct them with equal promptness.

The best decision I have made since assuming my post was my appointment of Deryck Maughan as Chief Operating Officer of Salomon Brothers Inc. He, along with the management of Phibro, join me in a pledge to make Salomon Inc a company that produces superior results for clients, employees and owners.

Annex VI

Alex Gorsky (Johnson & Johnson)

National Academy Foundation 2014

On behalf of Johnson & Johnson, I want to thank you for this honor. I greatly admire the work the National Academy Foundation has done and still does for the education, the careers and the lives of students like those of you here and thousands and thousands of others. Congratulations on the work you do for these young people.

I also want to congratulate you young people ... for how much you will do for us, for our companies, for our communities and for our world.

Johnson & Johnson is a pretty big company. But our company's aspiration is even bigger ... to help people everywhere in the world live longer, healthier and happier lives. That's a tall order, I know.

To live up to that promise requires commitment, talent and constant innovation. Not just new medicines and medical devices or consumer products, but innovation in everything we do in our company. We believe we can always do better and create a better outcome.

At Johnson & Johnson, we've learned that innovation is a direct result of collaboration – among our employees and scientists, health care professionals, academics and others.

The best collaboration is dependent on a diversity of individuals, ideas, approaches, values, dreams and hunches.

Diversity of thought is the spark that starts the engine of innovation.

So, for very selfish reasons, I'm very glad that the National Academy Foundation puts this time, effort and money into your future. We need you. We need your brains. We need your ideas and individuality. We need your creativity and your wildest daydreams. That's what will allow the next medical miracle, the next new vaccine, the next incredible medical device, and our next consumer product breakthrough. I'm not clairvoyant ... but one thing I can predict for sure about our future. If you kids win, we all win.

Annex VII

John Stumpf (Wells Fargo)

Q2 2014 Results

Thank you for joining us today. The second quarter was another strong quarter for Wells Fargo. We earned $5.7 billion in the quarter by our continued focused on creating long-term shareholder value to meeting our customers' financial needs including growing loans and deposits and deepening our relationships with our customers.

Let me highlight our growth during the second quarter compared with a year ago. We generated earnings of $5.7 billion, up 4% from a year ago and earnings per share up $1.01 per share, up 3% from a year ago. We had strong and broad based loan growth and our core loan portfolio is up $51.3 billion or 7%. Our credit performance continued to improve with total net charge-offs down $435 million or 38% from a year ago, and our net charge-off ratio was only 35 basis points annualized on average loans. Our outstanding deposit franchise continues to generate strong growth. With total deposit up $97 billion or 9%. We've grown deposits by an average of $265 million everyday over the past year. We deepened relationships across our company. Retail banking cross-sell was 6.17 products per household. Wholesale banking cross-sell was 7.2 products and wealth, brokerage and retirement cross-sell was 10.44 products. We reduced expenses from a year ago while we continue to invest in our businesses including strengthening our risk management infrastructure.

We also follow through our commitment to maintain strong capital ratios while returning more capital to shareholders. In the second quarter we increased our common stock dividend by 17% and continued to reduce our share count. We returned our net $3.6 billion to shareholders in the second quarter, up significantly from $1.6 billion a year ago. I am also proud that during the second quarter Wells Fargo was ranked the most respected bank in the world and the 11th most respected company overall according to Barron's Magazine 2014 ranking of the world's most respected companies. This recognition is a result of our dedicated team members remaining focused on our consistent vision and their commitment to meeting our customers' financial needs.

Annex VIII

Jeff Immelt (General Electric)

General Electric's new center will create 1,100 jobs in Detroit.

Speech in 2009.

Thank you all very much. I come to the Economic Club because of your kind invitation and come to Michigan because of its proud heritage and its promising future.

I believe that Michigan can partner with GE to create the next wave of economic progress. That's why earlier today, I stood with your governor and US Senators to announce a major new investment in your state.

General Electric's Manufacturing Technology and Software Center will be built right here and bring over 1,100 new jobs to Michigan. The engineers in our Van Buren Township facility will be developing technologies that can change peoples' lives clean energy, better transportation, affordable healthcare. Workers who might have made cars in the past will be bringing GE technology to life rebuilding our economy.

The people of this great state have been told that the decline of their manufacturing base was inevitable. I reject that pessimistic view. I believe that good jobs can again return to Michigan and in manufacturing centers across America.

Change can come, but it requires a new way of thinking. It requires a clear and determined plan of action. It requires a stiff dose of candor about the troubles we face, many of which we brought on ourselves. It requires leaders throughout the economy to take command of events.

The world has been reset. Now we must lead an aggressive American renewal to win in the future.

I am proud to work at GE, a great American company since the 1800s. Since I joined the company in 1982, GE has earned $230 billion more than any enterprise in the world. We have paid $130 billion in dividends to our investors again, more than any company in any country. Today, we have over 300,000 global employees with about half here in the United States.

We are the oldest remaining company in the Dow Jones Industrial Average. This is not because we are a perfect company; it is because we adapt. Through the years, we have remained productive and competitive. We have globalized the company, while investing massive amounts in technology, products and services. We know we must change again.

When the current economic unraveling began, many hoped it was merely a harsher version of past cycles. But now it's clear that a serious and difficult transformation is at hand, not just another turning of the wheel.

Think about it: For the first time since 1940, the economic output of all nations combined will actually shrink. Many scholars are at work on an extended analysis of the financial crisis. Yet it's not too soon to draw some conclusions about what went wrong, and what leaders can do to set things right.

Throughout my career, America has seen so much economic growth that it was easy to take it as a given. We prospered from the productivity of the information age. But, we started to forget the fundamentals and lost sight of the core competencies of a successful modern economy. Many bought into the idea that America could go from a technology-based, export-oriented powerhouse to a services-led, consumption-based

147

economy and somehow still expect to prosper.

That idea was flat wrong. And what did we get in the bargain? We've seen a great vanishing of wealth. Our competitive edge has slipped away, and this has hit the middle class hard.

As a nation, we've been consuming more than we earn, saved too little and taken on far too much debt. Growth in research and development has slowed. Our country has made too little progress on some of the defining challenges of our time like clean energy and affordable health care. Our budget and trade deficits have reached levels that are clearly not sustainable.

While some of America's competitors were throttling up on manufacturing and R&D, we deemphasized technology. Our economy tilted instead toward the quicker profits of financial services. While our financial services business has performed well, I can't tell you that we were entirely free of these errors. We weren't.

What has been the impact? Unemployment is at the highest point in 26 years. And, as a percentage of S&P 500 earnings, financial services expanded from 10 to 45 percent over a quarter-century.

Compensation systems have fallen out of balance. You know something is wrong when a mortgage broker is pulling down $5 million a year while a Ph.D. chemist is earning $100,000. Average real weekly wages have declined since 1980, meaning that we have been unable to provide a rising standard of living for the majority.

Leaders missed many opportunities to add to the capabilities of America. In 2000, the U.S. had a positive trade balance of high-tech products. By 2007, our trade deficit of the same products reached $50 billion. We have already lost our leadership in many growth industries, and other new opportunities are at risk. Trust in business is badly shaken, and it is going to take awhile to get it back.

This is unacceptable. Our country was built on great undertakings that brought out the best in government and business alike. But that kind of vision, that kind of focus on essential national goals, has been missing.

So let's work on a new strategy for this economy. We should clear away any arrogance, false assumptions, or a sense that things will be "ok" just because we are America. Rather, we should dedicate ourselves to be the most competitive country in the world.

GE believes in the benefits of free markets. Some of our greatest prospects are found in places like China and Brazil. More than half of our revenue is outside the U.S. But despite our global aspirations, GE shares a vital responsibility for the long-term competitiveness of this country.

Recently my colleague Peter Loescher, the CEO of Siemens, extolled the importance of Germany as an exporting country. In my career, I have never heard an American CEO say that the United States should be leading in exports. Well, I am saying it today: This country ought to be, and we can be, not just the world's leading market but a leading exporter as well.

GE plans to lead this effort. We have restructured during the downturn, adjusting to the market realities. At the same time, we are increasing our investments. We plan to launch more new products during this downturn than at any time in our history. We will sell these products in every corner of the world. We are creating a better company coming out of this reset.

Similarly, America needs a dramatic industrial renewal. We have to move forward on five fronts.

First: We need to significantly increase investment in research and development from an all-time low of 2 percent of the GDP. The only way to sustain a real competitive advantage is to invest in the needs of tomorrow.

GE has never forgotten the importance of R&D. Each year, we put six percent of our industrial revenue back into technology so much that more than half of the products we sell today didn't even exist a decade ago. As a consequence, we are a huge exporter.

The federal government has always been an important contributor to innovation. But federally supported R&D, as a percentage of GDP, has been declining since 1985. In the stimulus bill, we have increased basic research funding for the first time in recent memory. This trend should continue. But we need other improvements as well.

Engineering has been underemphasized in this country for a generation. Our high schools fall far short of the mark in science and math. This helps explain why only four percent of American college students have chosen engineering as a profession. If we're going to be serious about innovation in this country, then we've got to do a much better job training the next generation of innovators. At GE, we've dedicated 40 percent of our philanthropic giving about $150 million over the past five years to improving math and science capabilities in targeted city schools.

At the same time, American companies must reinvigorate their technical efforts. GE is a big funder of basic and applied research. We have filed more than 20,000 patents this decade. In addition, we have partnered with dozens of start-ups, adding to our technical capability.

Technology is what makes people and countries feel wealthy.

Technology is also the source of competitive advantage. In the past 25 years, GE has invested $20 billion in building better aircraft engines. We have created high-paying jobs and are a major exporter. Just last week, we received the largest order in our history from Etihad Airways, based in Abu Dhabi. The world demands this technology, and we're filling the need.

An American renewal will be built on technology. GE's R&D budget has not been cut. And that's a course of action I'd recommend to every company that wants to get through the economic crisis even stronger than before.

Second: America should get busy addressing the two biggest global

150

challenges – clean energy and affordable health care. In the future, we can have far greater energy diversity and security, while reducing global warming. In the future, we can also reduce health care inflation. All of this is within our reach.

For decades now, the most vital of commodities has been largely left to the control of others. The price for these commodities will rise due to increased consumption in emerging markets. We're in for terrible risks if we follow this path of increased dependency. At the same time, the science of climate change has become more certain. It's essential that we create a position of affordable, clean and secure energy for America.

In 2005, we launched an initiative we call Ecomagination. We've made a business decision to focus all the innovative powers of GE to solving the problems of energy use and environmental stewardship.

We've brought to market 75 new products to help our customers benefit from renewable technology through serious reductions in the cost and use of energy. We've dramatically reduced our own carbon footprint. In only four years' time, our revenues from environmentally friendly technology have nearly quadrupled to $17 billion.

We have focused our engineers on innovation in renewable energy, biofuels and battery technology. We are a leader in Smart Grid technology, which will empower consumers to save on their energy bills.

We believe that technology will help us make better use of old energy sources. In Indiana, GE and Duke Energy are building the largest-scale coal gasification plant in the world. We are also making a substantial investment in nuclear power. To provide clean, low-cost energy in a growing economy, I believe that nuclear and coal power will be absolutely essential.

Solving the clean energy challenge will create broad economic opportunity in this country. Our Ecomagination initiative has created tens of thousands of jobs at GE and in our supply chain. If the U.S. would drive a renewable energy standard of 12 percent by 2012 up from

5 percent it is today we would create 250,000 green jobs in the economy.

In health care, we're looking at an industry challenged by rising costs, poor access, and persistent quality issues. If we're not ready for the immense challenges coming our way on health care, the economic consequences would be devastating.

In large part it's a challenge of cost, and one sure way to attack that problem is with steady, focused investment to bring forth innovation. This year, my company launched an initiative called Healthymagination. We've committed to investing $6 billion in health care advances that will lower our customers' costs, broaden access to care, and increase the quality of outcomes.

We will launch 100 products at lower price points, such as a handheld ultrasound which will someday replace the stethoscope. And we are moving our capability into the underserved population in areas like infant care and mammography.

Aligning the American renewal with the challenges of energy and health care will keep our country on the leading edge. There is no question whether there will be breakthroughs in these areas just by who and when. The leader in these fields will dominate the global economy in the decades that come.

Third: We must make a serious commitment to manufacturing and exports. This is a national imperative. We all know that the American consumer cannot lead our recovery. This economy must be driven by business investment and exports.

We should set a national goal to create high value added jobs and have manufacturing jobs be no less than 20 percent of total employment, about twice what it is today. And we should commit ourselves to compete and win with American exports.

I've had people explain to me the Darwinian nature of markets. They tell me that America has seen a natural evolution from farming to manufacturing to services. After all, they say, this has happened in other mature economies. But there is nothing predestined or inevitable about the industrial decline of the U.S., if we as a people are prepared to reverse it.

We would do much better to observe the example of China. They've been growing fast because they invest in technology and they make things. They have no intention of letting up in manufacturing in order to evolve into a service economy. They know where the money is and they aim to get there first.

America has to get back in that game. As I said earlier, it starts with a strong core of innovation. But we also need a financial system that is built around helping industrial companies to succeed. GE is an important part of this financial services approach. We plan to focus GE Capital on financing small- and medium-sized customers in industries that we know the best.

America is in great need of an updated manufacturing infrastructure. This means better roads and airports; pervasive broad-band capability; and a bigger and smarter electricity grid. Old factories can become more productive with upgraded infrastructure.

The other secret to manufacturing competitiveness is a well-trained team. Annually, we invest $1 billion in training. All of our training has some impact on the factory floor. It used to take us 100 days to make a locomotive; now we can do it in 20. Through the use of lean manufacturing techniques, our 100-year-old Erie factory can export to Mexico and Brazil. Operational capability is a core part of GE's strategy.

In some areas, we have outsourced too much. We plan to "insource" capabilities like aviation component manufacturing and software development. These are the things we will be working on in Michigan. This will make us faster and more competitive over the long term.

We recently made the decision to build new capability in our appliances plant in Louisville, adding 420 new jobs. These workers will build an

153

innovative, hybrid water heater that uses 50 percent less energy. We could have made this product in China. But our Louisville team has committed to quality and productivity standards that make them competitive. We can serve our customers with speed and quality. We can make the same profit by manufacturing in the U.S., and our team deserves their chance to compete.

It is time, as well, for a new era of labor-management relations. The last generation has been tougher on workers. They have been poorly served by union leadership and management alike, and this must change.

We've been avoiding some hard truths. We pretend that high-cost systems work in a global economy; they don't. We believe that American consumers care where things are made; they don't. We believe that managers can move work wherever we want without consequence; that is foolish. In the fight between unions and management, the worker has suffered.

One of GE's most productive manufacturing plants is in South Carolina, where we make gas and wind turbines. We are one of the State's biggest employers. We have invested billions in long-term product leadership. Engineers and production workers are on the same team. A production worker earns a great salary because they are winning around the world. Their biggest customer is Saudi Electric Corporation.

In any industry, workers and management share a fundamental interest in the success of the enterprise. And to advance that common interest, we have to be more honest and flexible about what it takes to compete.

The renewal of American industry will require us to be globally competitive exporter. Business should reinvest in new American jobs which will create leadership in the future. That is why we are here today.

Fourth: We should welcome the government as a catalyst for leadership and change.

I'm a free-market guy I believe in the endless possibilities of individual

154

choice and private initiative. But this isn't the first time that business and government have had to work together for national ends. We should work together again today, setting goals for productivity, job creation and exports.

There's a long history in this country of government spending that prepares the way for new industries that thrive for generations. Think of the NIH or NASA, and all the new innovations that came out of these programs from computing to communications to healthcare.

America has that kind of chance with unprecedented levels of new government investment. Congress and the Administration have decided to invest in job creation, and the amounts of money involved can make a big difference not just by putting people to work, but also by aligning with basic national purpose.

The key is making sure those hundreds of billions of dollars fall on the fertile ground of innovation, and not bureaucracy. We need to see this new spending for what it is: an opportunity to turn financial adversity into national advantage to launch innovations of lasting value to our country.

It has always been a certainty that information technology could improve quality and lower cost in health care. To date, the applications have been poorly implemented, and the hospitals that need investment the most have been unable to afford newer systems.

The stimulus has set aside $20 billion for new health care systems. This reinvestment, along with the quality standards that accompany it, will transform health care.

The stimulus is a real opportunity to accelerate investment during the downturn to create long-term growth. This is all upside.

At the same time, we are going to get more regulation. And this could be dangerous. The administration has proposed financial regulation, tax reform and health care reform. Quite honestly, some of the policies I have seen concern me about the long-term impact on economic growth.

But business must engage, because status quo is not an option. The country has massive problems and social unrest. Fighting to protect the past is just wrong.

I recently joined President Obama's economic recovery advisory board. He can count on my openness and honesty. More importantly, he can count on GE's support to drive competitiveness and innovation that will improve the economy.

The challenges we face won't be solved by the free market alone. But through a real public-private partnership, we can dramatically improve America's competitiveness. Today, people in this country want to see business and government work together.

An American renewal will be shaped by the public and private sectors, and more than ever by a willingness to act boldly for the good of the country.

Fifth: It is possible for a global business leader to also be a good citizen.

The primary job of business leaders is to build competitive companies that win over the long term in every corner of the world. To do that, business must shake off the short-term mindset that brought on so many problems. We can't blame Wall Street. We must have the courage to invest and we must do it now.

We must set compensation policies that reward long-term growth in earnings and cash generation. More important, compensation should reflect company success. At GE, the company always comes first. I want GE people to "keep score" based on creating value through our innovation. Our success is institutional and transcends individual gain.

We must partner in our communities. Big business should work with smaller companies in our supply chain to help them compete globally. And we should partner with local governments to fix our education system.

In the end, business leaders are accountable for the competitiveness of their own country. We must say so publicly. This will not hurt our ability to globalize. Rather, I think it will make other countries admire our business leaders more. We must end the impression that American CEOs are short-term speculators.

Protectionist sentiment is growing in the U.S. But protectionism is not the answer. If other countries follow this trend and many have started to react, including China opportunities will vanish. Business leaders can help the country be competitive again. And out of this competitiveness will come a more self-confident society.

I want GE to be a great company. A great company keeps its eye on problems that need solving. A great company builds alignment from factory floor to the boardroom. A great company recognizes that an American strategy is part of a global strategy. A great company invests in the future. Great companies must be a part of the American renewal. There's room for any enterprise that aligns itself with needs that are basic, and needs that are vast. This is our vision for GE.

On a personal note, I would hate to think that the lasting impression of American business is the one that exists today. We can do better. We have made our companies globally competitive; now we must do the same for our country. We can help to solve some of these difficult problems and create an optimistic future.

I am excited about our future together. I embrace the promise of this investment in Michigan. I am also energized by the challenges that face GE. Not because the economy is good, but because the challenges we face will inspire the type of new thinking that is required in the future.

Over the last generation, Americas "service strategy" was too weak and our goals were too low. This approach must be abandoned. In its place, we should create an American Industrial Renewal by moving on five fronts: invest in new technology; win where it counts in clean energy and affordable health care; become a country that is good at manufacturing and exports; embrace public-private partnerships; and promote leaders who are also good citizens.

157

From economic chaos we will create new opportunities for the people of this city and this country. We will once again be prosperous, but more importantly, we will be proud.

It is time to think big again. We must hold ourselves to a higher standard and we must renew America's economy to embrace the same kind of dream that transformed this city and this world not so long ago.

Let's commit ourselves to begin that work today. Thank you.

Annex JX

Severin Schwan (Roche Holding)

Annual General Meeting

Roche Holding Ltd

1 March 2011

Address by Severin Schwan

Chief Executive Officer

Fellow Shareholders, Ladies and Gentlemen,

I, too, extend a warm welcome to you to this year's Annual General Meeting.

2010 wasn't an easy year for Roche, yet it was still a successful year in various ways. There are

three main topics I would like to discuss:

• Firstly: The financial results for 2010 and the outlook for the current business year.

• Secondly: The significance of our Group-wide Operational Excellence initiative for our

long-term innovation strategy, and where it stands now.

• And thirdly: How we are advancing personalised healthcare and what this means for

patients; I will be illustrating this point with a specific example.

First of all I would like to briefly review our key financial results for 2010.

If we look at our sales growth, we see that two exceptional factors significantly influenced the

Group result in 2010:

• Firstly, sales of our flu medication Tamiflu fell sharply as anticipated (down 2.3 billion

Swiss francs from 2009). This was because we had already supplied most of the

pandemic-driven orders to governments by early 2010 and the flu season was relatively

mild last year.

• Secondly, exchange-rate movements – especially the weakness of the euro and dollar

versus the (strong) franc – had a strong negative impact on our result in Swiss francs.

Excluding sales of Tamiflu, Group sales (and Pharmaceutical sales) advanced 5% in local

currencies. In the Diagnostics Division, sales advanced by 8%. The sales growth of both

Divisions significantly outpaced the market.

Thanks to synergies gained from the Genentech integration and cost-control measures, we also

160

enhanced our earning power. The Group's operating profit grew faster than sales, rising by a

robust 7% to 16.6 billion Swiss francs in local currencies. Profitability (operating margin)

improved further in both Divisions accordingly.

Consolidated net income rose 4% to 8.9 billion Swiss francs versus 2009, largely due to the

strong operating result.

We succeeded in our objective of achieving a double-digit rise in Core Earnings per Share,

which advanced 10% in local currencies.

Roche owes its success to its employees. Thanks to their tremendous dedication and hard work,

we once again achieved our goals last year, despite an increasingly challenging market

environment. On behalf of the entire Executive Committee, I would like to thank all our

employees for their important contributions.

We anticipate low single-digit sales growth in local currencies for Group and Pharma this year

(excluding Tamiflu sales, which are hard to predict). Naturally, this forecast also reflects the

effects of healthcare reform in the US and European cost-saving measures.

Overall, we expect Pharmaceutical sales to advance in line with market growth. Meanwhile,

Diagnostics Division sales are expected to significantly outpace the market again.

Cost-cutting programs in industrialized countries alone will squeeze sales and operating

profit by an additional half a billion Swiss francs this year. Despite an increasingly challenging

market environment and the introduction of an excise duty in the US, we have set ourselves the

objective of a high single-digit increase in Core Earnings per Share at constant exchange rates.

In view of growing pricing pressures, increasingly stringent approval requirements and the

setbacks in our development pipeline, in November 2010 we launched the comprehensive

Group-wide Operational Excellence initiative.

Operational Excellence is designed to strengthen the Group's productivity and innovation

capacity and thereby secure Roche's long-term success.

The greatest changes will be in the Pharmaceuticals Division, where we will be adjusting our

global sales organization, taking steps to improve efficiency and productivity in product

development, and optimizing our manufacturing network. Implementation of Operational

Excellence is already under way and will continue through 2012. We expect to achieve savings of 2.4 billion Swiss francs annually from 2012 on. As previously announced, the initiative will

involve the elimination of about 4,800 positions out of a global workforce of roughly 82,000 (at

the time when we announced Operational Excellence).

A total of 530 jobs will be lost in Switzerland. I should mention at this point that we currently

employ over 10,000 people in Switzerland and have created around 1,600 additional positions in

the last five years alone. And I am confident that solid growth in the future will enable us to

create new positions again, also here in Switzerland.

Our Operational Excellence program is on track. In other words, the majority of employees

affected have been personally informed. We have also re-prioritized projects in research and

development where necessary and initiated the divestiture of manufacturing sites as planned.

It was very important for us from the outset to find socially responsible solutions for the affected

employees. So I am glad that it has been possible to conclude social compensation plan

negotiations in Switzerland and elsewhere successfully and amicably.

This initiative is not just about cutting costs; we are taking these measures proactively from a

position of strength with a view to setting the right priorities for a successful future. This will

give us the financial flexibility we need going forward, to be able to invest substantial funds in

healthcare innovations. It will also enable us to secure our long-term growth and profitability so

that Roche remains attractive for investors. Making sure that Roche remains an employer of

choice is also an important priority for me. Operational Excellence will help keep Roche on track

for success, which will in turn ensure that Roche remains a great place to work for its many

thousands of employees.

We will continue to focus primarily on helping patients through our outstanding achievements in

science. Roche employs twenty thousand highly qualified people (a quarter of the workforce) in

R&D alone, and 3,000 of these work in Basel.

Roche stands out in the pharmaceutical industry for its expertise in personalized healthcare.

Indeed, personalized healthcare paradigms increasingly shape our research and development

programs.

Our success is based on our single-minded pursuit of innovation. We seek to develop medicines

and diagnostics that create tangible added value for physicians and patients alike in therapeutic areas with high unmet medical need. (Here in Basel alone we invest around two billion Swiss

francs annually in research into metabolic and central nervous system disorders.) However,

advances in medicine and pharmaceuticals carry inherent risks, as we were again reminded last

year.

But the setbacks we experienced were matched by important R&D successes. Our research and

development pipeline counts as one of the strongest in the industry, both for diagnostics and

pharmaceuticals. We currently have 102 projects in our Pharma development portfolio - 62 new

drugs and 40 additional indications – that are being tested in clinical trials involving around

330,000 patients around the world.

Just a few weeks ago, for example, we were pleased to report results from a third phase III trial

showing that our leading cancer medication Avastin significantly improved progression-free

survival in ovarian cancer. Every year, an estimated 230,000 women worldwide are diagnosed

this disease. Based on the excellent clinical trial results, Roche has submitted a European Union

marketing authorization application and plans to file for approval in the US before the end of this year.

Our priorities for the near term are our projects in late-stage clinical development, including (as

the chart shows) twelve new molecular entities in five different therapeutic areas. We are

confident that these projects will provide a solid basis for our future growth.

Insights from modern molecular diagnostics mean it is now possible to fit treatments more

precisely to patient needs. Of the twelve new molecules I just referred to, half are designed for

targeted use in specific patient populations (with the help of companion diagnostic tests).

…including six personalized therapies

We have made huge strides in personalized healthcare in recent years. Vemurafenib, our BRAF

inhibitor for skin cancer, MetMAb for lung cancer, T–DM1 and pertuzumab for breast cancer,

and other projects in virology and inflammatory disease – all these molecular entities, together

with their companion diagnostics, represent major advances for patients.

Our targeted diagnostic and therapeutic options are helping us to fulfil our promise of offering

patients and physicians significant clinical benefits in terms of efficacy, quality and safety. These

therapies are not only more focused in their efficacy, and therefore more cost-effective – which

has significant economic benefits for regulators and payers – they also improve patients' quality

of life, prolong survival by several years in some cases, and can even save lives if administered

when a disease is in its early stages.

Last year I presented one of these six late-stage development projects to you in more detail,

notably vemurafenib (RG7204), a BRAF inhibitor designed to treat a specific type of aggressive

malignant melanoma. Perhaps you remember Michael Roberts, the 72-year old skin cancer

patient whose story we showed in a short documentary. This is a man who, at the end of 2009,

had been given only a few weeks to live. I am delighted to be able to inform you today that (all

things considered) Michael Roberts is still doing well. Early last year he even started competing

in triathlons again!

The latest trial data on vemurafenib, published earlier this year, confirm its positive effect. A

clinical study showed for the first time that a personalized medicine used to treat this aggressive

form of skin cancer is able not only to substantially improve patients' quality of life but also

prolong survival. Roche is now working closely together with healthcare authorities worldwide

so that patients do not have to wait any longer to be treated with this drug. We will soon be

filing for approval in the USA, followed by other countries. This is a striking example of the way

in which personalized healthcare is gradually becoming a reality.

The revolutionary advances we are starting to see in molecular biology give us a clear strategic

edge across a number of areas, including our ability to raise research (and development)

productivity.

I would like to conclude this section by talking about two other candidate products at an

advanced stage of development in our personalized healthcare portfolio: T-DM1 and

pertuzumab – both of which are used to treat HER2-positive breast cancer, a particularly

aggressive form of the disease.

Breast cancer is the most common cancer in women worldwide (and the second most common

cancer altogether). One in ten women develop this type of cancer at some stage in their lives,

and more than 1.4 million new cases are diagnosed each year. Despite major advances in

treatment, over 450,000 patients die of breast cancer each year, including 1,400 in Switzerland alone.

The battle against cancer is a tough one given the complexity of human biology. But it is one in

which we are steadily advancing in small steps (that mean big benefits for patients). Breast

cancer is a case in point. Thanks to decades of research, treatment options have advanced

enormously. I would now like to show you a simplified diagram illustrating how Roche is getting

a grip on breast cancer, and aims to beat it in the end.

Let's take a trip back in time to the seventies, when chemically (i.e. synthetically) produced

drugs represented a quantum leap in the treatment of diseases such as cancer. Over the next

few decades, chemotherapy remained the standard treatment regimen for cancer.

However, as is commonly known, chemotherapy agents are "non-specific", that is to say, they

attack healthy cells as well as cancerous ones. This often causes major side effects (such as hair

loss, nausea and weakening of the immune system) and therefore significantly compromises

quality of life.

At the end of the nineties, Roche achieved a huge breakthrough in cancer treatment with its

biopharmaceutical drug Herceptin. Back then, Herceptin was the world's first therapeutic

antibody for the targeted treatment of breast cancer, and it has since become a prime example

of personalized healthcare. The drug is only effective in patients whose tumors carry a

particular genetic defect, causing them to overproduce a protein called HER2. HER2-positive

tumors are highly aggressive, fast-growing, and likely to relapse. Around 20% of all women

with breast cancer have HER2-positive tumors, which means Herceptin can only be used in

conjunction with a companion diagnostic test.

Herceptin binds to HER2 receptors and blocks them, much like a key fitting into lock. Since the

HER2 protein is not overproduced in healthy cells, Herceptin only attacks cancer cells. However,

Herceptin is most effective when administered together with chemotherapy, which of course

also means side effects.

Building on the success of Herceptin, we are now working to develop and bring to market the

next generation of targeted treatments for HER2-positive cancer.

T-DM1, an antibody–drug conjugate in late-stage development, represents an entirely novel

approach to treating cancer. Simply put, it links the mode of action of Herceptin with the

170

targeted administration of chemotherapy. The same antibody used in Herceptin binds to the

HER2 receptors of the cancer cells. In addition, however, our researchers have now succeeded

in binding a highly potent chemotherapy agent directly to the antibody. This chemotherapy

agent is then introduced selectively into the cancer cells, which it destroys without harming

healthy cells. We therefore call this medicine an "armed" antibody.

T-DM1 is currently being evaluated in studies in women with advanced HER2-positive breast

cancer. The results so far are very promising: Firstly, women who no longer have any other

treatment options (i.e. whom Herceptin no longer helps) have responded to this drug. Secondly,

patients tolerate it significantly better: compared with conventional chemotherapy, the side

effect burden is halved.

In a few moments I will give you a closer insight into the significance of T-DM1 for patients in

another short documentary.

Another novel biopharmaceutical agent in our late-stage pipeline is pertuzumab. Unfortunately,

in many cases, cancer is resistant to existing treatments. Cancer cells are smart, find new ways

of evading attack and often begin to multiply again further down the line. Combination therapies

that can keep the cancer in check from several sides simultaneously are thus set to play an

increasingly important role.

Previous trials have shown that pertuzumab in combination with Herceptin and chemotherapy

improves the patient response rate by more than 50% (compared with Herceptin and

chemotherapy).

We will continue to strive to make good treatments even better, drawing on the new insights we

are gaining in molecular biology. Our goal is to transform cancer more and more into a chronic

disease instead of the fatal one it has usually been until now.

I would now like to show you a short documentary about what T-DM1 means for patients with

advanced breast cancer, and for their families. It features an American lady called Chris Tury,

who gives a moving account of her experiences.

The conference you just saw took place a year ago – which is a long time for women with

aggressive breast cancer. So we are particularly delighted that Chris Tury is still doing well. She

has been treated successfully with T-DM1 for the past three years.

T-DM1 and pertuzumab are specific examples of how our focus on scientific excellence is

achieving significant advances for patients. If the approval process goes to plan, we will be able

to launch both new medicines (together with a tissue-based companion diagnostic test) in the

coming years.

We aim to build on successes like these and tackle cancer and other serious diseases with

targeted and thus more effective strategies.

All the signs are that 2011 will be an outstanding year for personalized healthcare. And of one

thing I am sure: personalized healthcare has tremendous potential for patients, for healthcare

systems, and for Roche.

Thank you for your attention.

Annex X

Doug Mcmillon (Wal-Mart)

Picking up the Pace of Change for the Customer

Doug McMillon President & CEO, Wal-Mart Stores, Inc.

Walmart Shareholders Meeting 2014

William, I wanted to start with your story because you really went above and beyond for a customer. That is exactly what we're looking for. Thank you!

William represents what makes Walmart successful. It's our people. I've visited with so many of our associates around the world. And the thing that sticks with me is the pride you take in doing a good job. The care you take in serving our customers and in working together as a team.

This company has always been about our people. And it always will be.

My first Shareholders experience was in 1984. It was my very first day with Walmart, and, though I'd been hired to pick orders and load trailers in warehouse 2, they grabbed a few of the rookies and had us decorate the high school gym for the big meeting. And I thought that meeting was big.

I got to watch Sam lead several Shareholders meetings over the years. What I remember is his enthusiasm, his passion for this business, and

174

his love for our associates.

I learned from listening to him, and to Helen, what Walmart stands for. I saw him jump on stage before the meeting was supposed to start and just wing it. Well, we're a bit more buttoned up today but that passion is still here.

I've also learned about Walmart from Rob Walton, David Glass, Don Soderquist, Lee Scott, Mike Duke and countless other leaders. Some of them are here, and I'd like to ask our alumni to stand. Thank you all for what you helped to build. We won't let you down.

David Glass followed Sam Walton, and under his leadership we scaled up Supercenters and moved beyond the United States. He led us to incredible expansion and set the stage for more.

Lee Scott helped lead the company through amazing growth. He has been part of Walmart for 35 years and set us on a path toward becoming more sustainable.

And Mike, well, we should all be more like Mike: his strength of character, his ability to be a servant leader. Mike moved this company forward in the right way. He's leaving it stronger, more global, more focused on technology and the digital age. Thank you, Mike.

So, where are we today? More than 2 million associates. Just over 250 million customers a week. 27 countries. Multiple store formats and brands, and a host of ecommerce capabilities. And we're growing.

Over the last three years we've grown sales by $55 billion. We added $7.5 billion in net sales last year ... and 33 million square feet of retail space. We generated more than $10 billion in free cash flow.

This growth has allowed us to return more than $100 billion to our shareholders over the last 10 years. It's a record we are very proud of.

The foundation of our company is strong. We have dedicated, talented, and creative people, and we have the resources to become even stronger.

175

So, where do we go from here? I am excited about our future. There are so many new ways emerging to serve customers. Technology, data and information are opening new doors for us to lead through.

Our purpose of saving people money will always be relevant, but we'll do it in new ways.

A few core principles will guide our direction:

First, we will be a customer-driven company. We've always said the customer is our boss ...and we'll make decisions based on how we can serve them better.

Second, we will invest in our people. As we change and grow, it will be our associates who will make the difference.

Finally, we need to be at the forefront of innovation and technology. We will lead with urgency to get ahead of change.

With that as our foundation our plan is taking shape. We can think about it in three parts: now, new, and always. We need to get better at what we're already doing now. We also need to invent the new – to bring together the digital world of ecommerce with the physical world of our stores. And we will always stay true to Walmart's purpose and values.

Let's start with now. Every single one of us has a role to play in getting better right here, right now, today.

It's pretty straightforward – we need stores that customers want to shop... with merchandise they want to buy. Price leadership. Strong in stock. Friendly customer service. Compelling merchandise. Items that surprise and delight. Merchandise that is presented aggressively.

When we're at our best, the features in our stores anticipate what our customers want and need. They don't need a shopping list. They come in for basics, but they leave with new cushions for their patio set or a great new pair of shorts for summer. And they love doing it. It's fun! We must be stronger merchants, and we will work together to make it happen.

Developing New Capabilities

We will also develop new capabilities to serve customers in new ways. It is important that we all understand the shift that has happened in technology and retail, what it means for us, and what we're doing to win.

Let's start with a little show-and-tell. Think about the smart phone. It organizes our lives and rarely leaves our side. The best smartphones have 80,000 times as much processing power as the Apollo Guidance Computer that took Neil Armstrong and Buzz Aldrin to the moon.

Mobile has changed everything. People now spend more time on digital devices than they do watching TV. A lot of times, they're doing both at the same time.

At Walmart, we now get more ecommerce traffic in the U.S. from mobile devices than from desktop and laptop computers. And, increasingly, our customers will do their grocery shopping on their phone or tablet in their spare time, not during their precious family time. We're going to make that possible.

Now, what do you see?

This is a picture of one of our pick up points at a subway station in London where customers can collect items that they ordered. It may look like any other truck. But it offers access to 26,000 items today and who knows how many items and services tomorrow. This is just one example of the integration of digital and physical retail. Their device, our stores, and this new pick-up point.

You're familiar with megabytes and gigabytes and maybe even terabytes? Well, Walmart now has about 30 petabytes of shopping information. What on earth is a petabyte? One petabyte of digital music would play for 2,000 years. It's a lot.

For years, our data has helped us run our stores around the world. Now, it is helping us personalize the shopping experience in ways that let us

177

serve customers even better.

Let's look even further ahead. I'm sure you've heard of 3D printing. We've had some fun in the U.S. and the U.K. printing items for customers. Mostly, we've printed little mini-me's – small statues of themselves.

We can easily imagine a day when we can print small household items or replacement parts in a store or a DC. We can begin to envision a whole new way of delivering customized products to customers when and how they need them.

And, finally, think about this, associates starting with us today as teenagers have never known a world without the internet and mobile phones. Do you think they have new expectations for Walmart?

My point is that there's a lot of innovation and opportunity available to us. Customers will increasingly expect and require the best of both worlds. They want the excitement and the immediacy of shopping in a physical store and the freedom to shop whenever, however and wherever they want – to receive their merchandise the way they want. They want an experience that seamlessly adapts to their life.

All of this change is a good thing for us. Walmart can bring together our stores with new digital commerce capabilities to help customers save money, save time, and have access to what they want and need.

The opportunity is enormous. It feels like it's only limited by our imaginations.

Here's what our future may look like:

Our stores, 11,000 and growing, will provide access and convenience. If you need it right here, right now, we've got it. We will run great stores and clubs with great associates. You are our competitive advantage.

We'll keep adding services and pick-up points to our stores to become even more convenient.

We'll also strive to have collection points wherever our customers want us to be. Not only are we testing in tube stations in London but inside train cars in Toronto. Maybe someday we'll be near a school in Dallas, where a mom or dad is picking up their kids.

We've also seen the demand for food delivery, in places like the U.K., Mexico, and China. I recently visited our grocery delivery test in Denver. One of our customers described it like this. "It is like 'grocery fairies' suddenly arrived to make life easier for a busy Mom." "Grocery fairies"... I love that.

And of course, we'll keep improving our traditional ecommerce offering of ordering online and shipping to customers' homes.

To do all of this, we need to move – fast.

That's why we're piloting so many ideas around the world.

That's why we formed @WalmartLabs, hired more than 2,500 engineers, programmers and data scientists, and acquired 14 companies in the last three years. We recently became interested in a product search firm called Adchemy and bought it less than 3 months later. We focused on a wireless services provider named Simplexity and completed a deal 7 weeks later.

We can move fast. Walmart is picking up the pace of change to serve the customer better.

We're also building out our global fulfillment and replenishment network so we can get even closer to our customers. We're rolling out a new Global Technology Platform to provide a better customer experience on all devices.

And to bring all of this to life, we're investing in our people. I'm proud of the jobs and opportunities we offer, and we can do an even better job of creating opportunities to learn and grow. We'll prepare our associates to serve customers better, while building the careers you want at Walmart. I'm excited about the work underway in Walmart U.S.

179

because it is a critical part of our future.

So this is what real-time change looks like.

We will grow our same store sales, and we will grow with these new services, capabilities and locations to drive the top line. Customers will be able to access us through our stores and through their phones, tablets, websites and whatever comes next. Walmart will exceed their expectations!

Finally, let's talk about always – the things that are constant.

I'll start with our purpose. We save people money so they can live better. This is a noble pursuit. It's real. We help parents afford new clothes for school, put healthier meals on the table, and save for their child's education or a rainy day.

Our values won't change. Integrity, Service, Respect and Excellence. These are our guiding beliefs, and our behaviors will support those beliefs. Our culture is what makes us special. It's what makes us different. We must nurture it and reward those who live it.

And, as it relates to integrity, we are committed to conducting business in an ethical manner. Integrity is at the heart of everything we do. It's supported by our culture and the world class compliance and ethics capabilities we continue to strengthen. Doing the right thing, the right way, is the only way for us.

But we don't stop there.

We believe in Walmart's responsibility to lead on big issues, in big ways. It's one of the reasons many of us love being part of Walmart.

About 10 years ago, we began to understand that we could make a larger difference in the area of social and environmental sustainability. That period of learning was the beginning of a new era for us, and it really changed my personal perspective.

Ultimately, creating a more sustainable company is about people. It's about our customers, our associates, our kids and grandkids. We care about not only our own associates but also about the farmers and factory workers who make it possible for us to sell merchandise. We care about how they are treated and compensated. That's why we're investing to support additional training and safety.

We're focused, for example, on women. We're on track to help train 1 million women on farms and in factories, in technology, retail, and throughout the workforce. And we're ahead of schedule on sourcing $20 billion from women-owned businesses.

We'll also keep giving back in the communities we serve – whether that's through disaster relief or local manufacturing around the world or the millions of hours our associates volunteer each year.

As it relates to the environment, we've made terrific progress against our three big goals – to run on 100% renewable energy, to create zero waste, and to sell products that sustain people and the planet. I believe in those goals – as an associate and as a dad.

There are so many ways that Walmart can make a difference around the world. We're committed to doing just that. We will strengthen the trust we've established with customers and the communities we serve.

I want to close by speaking directly and personally to every Walmart associate. To every associate in this room. To every associate on the sales floor, the back room or in a DC. To every associate writing code or hauling freight.

I want you to feel the same excitement that I feel. I want you to see the same possibilities that I see. I want you to know in your heart, like I do, that our future is bright. We have the foundation and the people, and we know how we're going to win.

I know it's easy to look at everything that's going on and wonder what Sam would think about things like mobile apps, grocery delivery, or 3D printing.

So I'll leave you with a few words from Sam himself. He said:

"I've made it my own personal mission to ensure that constant change is a vital part of the Walmart culture itself. I've forced change sometimes for change's sake alone at every turn in our company's development. In fact, I think one of the greatest strengths of Walmart's ingrained culture is the ability to drop everything and turn on a dime."

Turn on a dime!

So what would Sam say about our opportunity? He'd say: go! He might even say: hurry up!

We won't let him down. Thank you.

About the Author

Dimitris Michas was born in Athens in 1987. He is a political communications specialist and a PhD candidate in nationalist rhetoric at the University of Athens. He studied Political Science and Public Administration at the University of Athens, Political Communication at the University of Glasgow, Southeast European Studies at the University of Athens and Business Administration at the University of Nicosia. He speaks six languages and has served as a communications consultant for international organizations and politicians.

www.ingramcontent.com/pod-product-compliance
Lightning Source LLC
Chambersburg PA
CBHW070928210326
41520CB00021B/6843